EMOTIONAL STORMS

Preventing Emotional Dysregulation in the Classroom

ANNE MAREE TANEY

First published by Ultimate World Publishing 2023
Copyright © 2023 Anne Maree Taney

ISBN

Paperback: 978-1-922982-72-8
Ebook: 978-1-922982-73-5

Cover design: Ultimate World Publishing
Layout and typesetting: Ultimate World Publishing
Editor: Marinda Wilkinson

Ultimate World Publishing
Diamond Creek,
Victoria Australia 3089
www.writeabook.com.au

ACKNOWLEDGEMENT OF COUNTRY

I respectfully acknowledge the Gkuthaarn and Kukatj people as the Traditional Custodians of the land on which this book was written. I recognise and honour their wisdom, strength and resilience and pay my respects to Elders, past, present and emerging. I acknowledge that the land was never ceded and always was, and always will be, Aboriginal land.

CONTENTS

DEDICATION

I dedicate this book to the children who
share their wisdom with me every day,
and their teachers, who continually inspire me.

To my family – you are my everything.
Your support and faith in my ability to undertake this
journey have made it possible.

INTRODUCTION

R iley's story: *It's Friday morning. I am exhausted. It has been another long term. Most students are doing their work, but two are restless – wandering around and annoying others. As I direct Jordan back to his work, I notice his eyes are wide, and his stance is defiant. I feel a stab of anxiety and predict trouble – but I must get him back on task. He is here to learn. My gut tells me this will not end well. And I am right. Jordan does not attempt to comply and answers back. Calmly, I repeat the instruction, giving him time to process the information and respond. But he doesn't. This interaction soon escalates to 'if you don't sit down and do your work, you must do it in your own time'. He knows this is the natural consequence of failing to complete his work. However, a stand-off emerges, ending with Jordan yelling, swearing and angrily kicking over a desk as he leaves the classroom. Not a great start to the day. I feel overwhelmed as I try to juggle the other students' needs and the curriculum's demands. And now I need to follow up with this one. Then there is the paperwork*

3

and dealing with his father, who will think it is my fault. Does it ever end? No lunch break today. Is it all worth it?

*All names in this book are made up. The stories reflect common themes but are fictional.

Many teachers will recognise Riley's feelings of overwhelm and the cascading fallout when a child dysregulates. Emotional storms not only take away from teaching and learning time, they add to the teacher's stress levels and contribute to burnout. The teacher's workload is already high – and these incidents compound it. Staff wellbeing is affected, and these emotional storms significantly impact other students. They should not witness aggression and violent behaviour during their school day. These incidents would be considered scary and potentially traumatic in another environment – *not* a regular occurrence. And then there is the child amid the storm. What led them to this place of vulnerability and dysregulation? Moreover, how could it have been avoided? What needs or skills are lacking? The wellbeing of all parties is at stake if we do not work to prevent emotional storms.

About 13 years ago, I completed a thesis entitled *The Social and Emotional Wellbeing of Students – The Perspective of Teachers*. At that time, my research revealed that most teachers believed they had little to no responsibility for their students' social and emotional wellbeing.[1] The belief was that students should turn up ready to learn – and they would teach the curriculum. Fortunately, this attitude is changing, but teacher education to support this change appears lacking. Compounding this is chronic time stress and staff shortages, which often prevent adequate investigation of the underlying causes of behaviours and may result in behaviour management practices that do little to change the situation. It is essential to seek out the reasons for a child's behaviour, as a child who gets labelled as 'difficult' or 'bad' in school has reduced lifetime opportunities, with the potential to pass this disadvantage on to the next generation.

In my work with Youth Justice and as a counsellor for children in schools, I have found an increasing demand for knowledge about behavioural issues and emotional regulation. Teachers *want* to understand the reasons behind children's behaviour as they feel powerless in the face of emotional storms and want better student outcomes.

This book provides practical and accessible strategies without focusing on a particular ideology, theory or program, as there is rarely a single story or a universal solution.

It provides broad knowledge to aid the recognition and prevention of emotional dysregulation. While the reader can explore each chapter independently to access specific information, I recommend reading the whole book initially to have the 'big picture'.

It is written understanding that teachers are time-poor and implementing different strategies for every child is impossible. Most strategies are brief, whole-of-class prevention activities that benefit the teacher and the class, while others you can ask teacher aides to assist with. There are also some you can train students to instigate themselves when needed, so they are empowered to manage their emotions in a connected and safe classroom.

Preventing emotional storms in the classroom will require embarking on an adventure that may include changes that are outside your comfort zone. When faced with change, our 'fight' or 'flight' system is often activated, and we resist suggestions out of hand. An open heart and an open mind are needed. Are you ready to take on this challenge? It is not for the faint-hearted – but the treasures you find will make the journey worthwhile.

Chapter 1 will start by looking at staff wellbeing and self-care. The Monash University study published in 2019 showed that one in five Australian teachers were concerned about their physical and psychological safety in the workplace, and 58% indicated that they intended to leave the profession within the next ten years.[2] Primary reasons identified included the workload, long hours worked, and the impact of work on health, wellbeing, family and relationships.[2] While self-care cannot fix these system issues – *and they do need fixing* – it can help you cope with these and the other stresses in your life. Maintaining or regaining your wellbeing is essential for you, your family, your friends and the students you teach. It is your anchor in the storm.

The second chapter introduces you to the child's navigation system – their brain – and how and when different parts develop. It also provides information about typical childhood development and the usual challenges encountered. Sometimes what we see as problematic behaviour is developmentally appropriate. Knowing this may not make it any less challenging for the adults in their lives, but it increases understanding and compassion.

As we progress through the book, you will see there are many things to be curious about and consider. Looking at Jordan's behaviour and subsequent emotional dysregulation through a developmental lens, we would wonder whether he has yet developed the executive functioning skills to allow him to sit still, maintain attention and manage impulsivity. If he hasn't, we need to teach these skills in an age-appropriate way; but for now, we need to avoid the storm.

The third chapter looks at neurodiversity, when navigation systems work differently. While many diagnoses fall under neurodiversity, this chapter focuses on attention deficit hyperactivity disorder (ADHD) and autism spectrum disorder (ASD), as these often cause significant challenges at school. It also includes foetal alcohol spectrum disorder (FASD), a pre-birth brain injury, as many strategies for ADHD and ASD are also effective for FASD. Understanding the diagnostic criteria and symptoms can give insight and an understanding of the child's behaviour and, therefore, keys to what may help prevent dysregulation.

While teachers do not suggest diagnoses to parents or others, they are excellent at noticing behavioural patterns, and this information will assist the child in accessing the most appropriate support.

Chapter 4 considers those children who live in the storm – those who have experienced developmental trauma or are experiencing ongoing trauma in their lives. Developmental trauma and adverse childhood experiences (ACEs) impact the developing brain and body, with potentially lifelong consequences for physical and mental health.[3] These children are likely to have a heightened threat response resulting in dysregulation with no apparent cause. A lack of knowledge about the potential impact of ACEs may mean that teachers inadvertently trigger or punish a child for their trauma.

Chapter 5 looks at how you can influence the weather. We are social creatures, and our brains connect, giving us enormous power if we use it purposefully. This chapter considers how you can use non-verbal communication and the tone, prosody, volume, and rate of your speech to maintain calm, transmit enthusiasm, promote connection and give a sense of safety in the classroom. When a child dysregulates, you have a choice – you can share your calm, or be sucked into their storm. To be in a position to be purposeful, you must look after your needs first.

Chapter 6 reflects on the importance of developing relationships with the students. Learning occurs within the context of a relationship making this a vital aim for teachers. The bonus is that managing behaviour and maintaining a calm classroom is much easier when children feel safe and connected. This chapter will look at the autonomic nervous system ladder as described by Deb Dana,[4] focusing on 'safe and social' and what aids students and teachers to stay in or return to this space. Without a relationship, your influence is limited. Neither Jordan nor Riley felt 'safe and social' after their interaction.

In Chapter 7, we look at the training teachers can implement before going to sea and encountering storms. These activities are real prevention work and will give children skills for life. The chapter will include everyday strategies that calm the amygdala. If you choose ones that fit with you, you are more likely to use them consistently, and you will also benefit. Pre-sea training also includes increasing emotional literacy. If children can say how they feel, it can negate the need to act it out.

Chapter 8 moves on to predicting storms. This chapter is about noticing the very early signs of things deteriorating. If you find the class (or you) are becoming restless, shut down or overwhelmed, do a five-minute regulation activity from the previous chapter. Your effort will be well rewarded. Using a whole-of-class strategy also avoids singling out a student whose emotions may heighten due to embarrassment. Some students go to 'fight', some go to 'flight', others will 'freeze', and still others will 'fawn' or people-please. People generally have a default mode when distressed, so knowing your students will help you identify potential storms. Riley had predicted a storm. He felt it in his gut, a part of the autonomic nervous system that 'feels' these things. Preventative action could have occurred then.

Chapter 9 examines the life rafts you can offer students with heightened emotions and how you can do this. For them to be effective, you must introduce these before any crisis. If you have ever tried to get a child to take slow, deep breaths when they are in 'fight or flight' mode, you will realise that it is doubtful that they will comply if this has not been something they have practised previously. A strong connection with students will make it more likely that they will climb on board the life raft and accept the help you offer.

Chapter 10 examines what to do when your early efforts have failed, or you have been busy with other students and have missed the signals. Sometimes, no matter what you do, a storm will eventuate, and you will need to ride the waves, maintain safety and give space and time. All storms pass. The best course of action is to stay calm and self-regulate. The time you invested in your self-care will see you through this storm and out the other side. This is true of students too – if pre-training occurred, when Jordan left the classroom and had calmed enough to think, he would know where to go to cool down.

Chapter 11 considers what to do after the storm – after the child (and you) have regulated. This chapter is about reconnecting and repairing the relationship and discussing how it could be different next time, including any learnings or consequences resulting from the incident.

And finally, in Chapter 12, you have made it through the storm and out the other side! This chapter is an opportunity to reflect on what you have done with what you have learnt. Change takes time and courage and can be chaotic, but you have taken a significant step. Your commitment to your class is inspirational.

Teachers and school staff contribute not only to education, but to the wellbeing of students every day, and I am passionate about supporting you in doing this. While Poseidon could control the weather and the seas, I am afraid I do not have those magic powers. Knowledge, however, is a power of a different kind – and compassion, connection and curiosity about the causes of emotional storms make a huge difference. There is also great power in humour and the use of symbolism and metaphor. This book aims to give you an understanding of the issues and some practical strategies to support you, no matter the weather. Trust yourself to experiment and adapt them – and most importantly, take care of yourself.

BEFORE YOU READ 'EMOTIONAL STORMS'

HOW DO YOU RATE YOUR:

Self-care ★★★★★

Knowledge of Childhood Development ★★★★★

Knowledge of Trauma and ACEs ★★★★★

Ability to Self-Regulate ★★★★★

Knowledge of Neurodiversity ★★★★★

Connection with your students ★★★★★

Knowledge of Emotional Regulation ★★★★★

Use of Prevention Strategies ★★★★★

Confidence to deal with Emotional Storms ★★★★★

Date:

CHAPTER 1

CHECK YOUR ANCHOR

Sonya's evening: *Another takeaway dinner. I feel so guilty – but I'm stuffed! Mentally and physically exhausted. Not sleeping, not exercising, and having no fun in my life. Just thinking about all I am doing wrong is overwhelming. I feel like I am a bad mum and an inadequate partner. I'm not sure I even want to go to work. However, I can't fix that now. I have planning and marking to do, the kid's lunches to make, and the washing needs to be done – before I can even think about sleep. Hopefully, tomorrow will be better. Fewer teachers will be away, and I can just have my own class. I may even get my student-free time. Ha! Not likely! The best I can hope for is no meltdowns and no fights. The meltdowns scare me. They leave me feeling on edge and waiting for the next explosion. I cannot deal with these extra stresses at the moment. It's best not to think about it. One more wine while I finish up. It will help me relax and sleep better.*

Increasing your knowledge and understanding of emotional storms and their origins will make you a better weather forecaster. However, if an unexpected storm blows in and you are not firmly anchored, you cannot be sure you can help anyone else. The stormy and unpredictable seas may soon overwhelm you. Your ongoing self-care is your anchor in the classroom. Self-care is necessary for everyone to manage life's stressors. However, the teaching profession has unique challenges and many systems and societal issues to contend with, which magnifies the need.

In a pre-COVID study conducted in Australia, 55% of teachers rated their job as *extremely or very stressful*.[5] COVID has exacerbated this in many ways. Teacher stress and burnout are global problems, with many teachers leaving or planning to leave the profession.[5] How can we change this? It is a big problem with no immediate answers; however, valuing teachers and looking after teacher and student wellbeing should be high on the political agenda. The students are the future of our nation, and teachers have enormous input into their lives – not only in what they teach but with the behaviour they model and the values they espouse. Promoting self-care and the other strategies in this book are not intended to solve broader issues or to lay the entire responsibility with teachers. The book suggests ways that individuals can make a difference in their lives, and those of their families and students, *despite* the difficulties. They present a way to thrive rather than survive in the face of significant challenges.

> *'As important as it is to have a plan for doing work, it is perhaps more important to have a plan for rest, relaxation, self-care and sleep.'*[6]

A lack of self-care reduces your ability to manage emotional storms in the classroom. Then, when a child dysregulates, you are more likely to join their storm, with your emotions escalating in response to their behaviour. Your heart starts racing, your muscles tense, and your breathing gets fast and shallow. Your body is preparing you for 'fight or flight'. You are then functioning in your emotional brain rather than your logical brain. At this point, you are more likely to do or say things that worsen the situation. You might even find yourself pressing their buttons in response to them pressing yours, leaving you feeling either defensive or remorseful afterwards. The fallout from these incidents can influence your relationship with the student and the rest of the class. Repetitive incidents can affect your mood and wellbeing, depleting your reserves of resilience. In the long term, high stress with no self-care can lead to burnout and mental health issues, impacting your family, personal relationships, and the quality of your work.

So, what is self-care? *Life in Mind* describes it this way:

> *'Self-care refers to activities that preserve and maintain one's physical, emotional and mental health. It is an ongoing commitment to look after yourself through helpful behaviours that protect your health during periods of stress.'*[7]

Essential supplies – Exercise, diet and sleep

Have you noticed that the basics of wellbeing – exercise, diet and sleep – are the first things to fall off the radar when you become stressed? If you are like me and many others, this is the case. Like Sonya, we get more takeaways, are too tired and lack the motivation to exercise, and sleep either becomes elusive or we sleep too much. These basics are also the first things we should attend to once we notice the boat is rocking and we risk getting swept overboard. Our mind and body are intimately connected, so looking after our physical health also impacts our emotional wellbeing and mental health. The no-frills bargain-basement anchor includes diet, sleep, exercise, water and a healthy work-life balance.

Knowing the precise requisites for staying anchored in wellbeing rather than having some vague idea about needing a good diet, sufficient exercise and adequate sleep is helpful. So, we will look briefly at what the experts say. While there are well-researched dietary guidelines, a practical guide for diet is Pollan's 'eat food, not too much, mainly plants'.[8] The distinction is that 'food' is 'real food' rather than food-like substances.[8] I found this appealed to my sense of humour, and I now appraise items in the supermarket as 'food' or 'food-like substances'. This recognition does not mean I do not eat them, but I am more aware of my choices. The Australian Guide to Healthy Eating recommends enjoying a wide range of foods from the five food groups and drinking plenty of water.[9]

Interestingly, different countries have slightly different guidelines reflecting different cultures' relationship to food groups. The Mediterranean approach includes wine in moderation and highlights that people should enjoy meals with others. However, I like the simplicity of Pollan's advice. Which guidelines fit with your way of life and culture? Think about your diet. Are there small ways you could improve it?

Many teachers (and parents) feel they do sufficient incidental exercise – but is it enough? The World Health Organisation (WHO) recommends 150 minutes of moderate-intensity aerobic exercise each week (i.e. 30 minutes 5 days/week) or 75 minutes of high-intensity exercise.[10] Some base their exercise on doing 10,000 steps a day, however, if these are not 'brisk' steps, they may not provide as much benefit as you think. The WHO defines moderate exercise as an exercise that increases your heart rate and makes you breathe faster.[10] This may include such activities as a brisk walk to work or the bus stop, mowing or gardening, or even playing your favourite music loud and dancing with the mop as you do the housework. They do not have to be consecutive minutes.

It could include the 10-minute aerobic activity you did with your students to expend their excess energy. This activity can tick boxes for your wellbeing and theirs, and get bonus points for creating connections through shared movement and having fun together. Taking time out and walking in the natural environment also has many additional benefits. Integrating exercise into our days can make our goals easier to achieve and not another time burden. While it can take a substantial effort to start regular exercise, the increase of hormones and chemicals, such as endorphins, dopamine and serotonin, makes it easier to continue. Rather than being tired, we often have more energy and enthusiasm for what we need to do after exercising.

We all have difficulty sleeping sometimes, but we must consider improving things when this becomes a regular pattern. The National Sleep Foundation Guidelines recommend that adults should sleep for 7–9 hours a night, but it is not just about the quantity – the quality is essential too.[11] The first step to improving our sleep is to check our 'sleep hygiene'. Some important things to note:

- Alcohol may initially make you sleepy and relaxed, but it interferes with sleep quality. You may go to sleep initially but then wake up and struggle to go back to sleep. Although people often drink alcohol to feel better, alcohol is a depressant.
- Caffeine is a stimulant and can make sleep difficult when consumed later in the day. Drinking coffee impacts some people more than others. Reducing your intake is a good first step if getting enough sleep is problematic.
- Research shows that, when used before bedtime, the blue light emitted from smartphones and eReaders may impact our sleep as it can disrupt the secretion of the hormone melatonin and affect the rhythm of our circadian clock.[12]
- A regular time for going to bed is helpful as we all have an inbuilt sleep/wake cycle. If we go past it, it can cause sleep

problems. Just like babies, if we get overtired, it can be challenging to get off to sleep.

- Guided relaxation recordings can be helpful.

If improving sleep hygiene does not work, you should seek professional advice. A chronic lack of sleep can impact your physical and mental health, and your ability to cope with life's ups and downs.

What makes the sun shine for you?

Activities considered 'self-care' are endless, but what is invigorating for one person may be draining and arduous to another. You should choose meaningful activities that fit your interests and bring you joy, and commit to making them a regular part of your life. The idea is for it to be an activity that gets you in the 'zone', where your focus is only on what you are doing. You are not worried about what you did yesterday or planning for tomorrow – you are in the present. These activities give you strength and resilience, the ability to bounce back from stress and crises. It also means your entire world does not revolve around work, providing better balance in your life and anchoring you in tough times.

It can be hard to plan ways to regain your wellbeing when stressed, even though you know you should do it. Getting the motivation and energy to think about options, let alone undertake any additional activity, is challenging, so I have suggested a process from Acceptance and Commitment Therapy to get you started. Acceptance and Commitment Therapy (ACT) is more than a type of therapy – it provides a values-based way of living.

A first step in this approach can be considering your values and how fully you live by them. When our actions reflect our values, we are at peace within ourselves. However, we are human, and there are often many conflicts between our values and what we do. By moving closer to our values, we will improve our wellbeing. Something important to you may be self-care itself, or it may fit better with another value, such as:

Creativity	Skilfulness	Growth
Fitness	Connection	Spirituality
Adventure	Excitement	Community
Learning	Altruism	Competitiveness
Fun	Mindfulness	Service

There are many more values, but those listed above lend themselves well to self-care activities. Next, establish a goal that reflects your chosen value and takes you toward the life you want to live. If fitness is your value, your goal may be to start walking regularly. This activity will meet the need for exercise and also uphold your value. If spirituality is your value, your goal may be to re-engage in spiritual activities that have brought you peace in the past. Using the SMART goals process can increase your motivation to follow through. A SMART goal in the ACT world is *Specific, Meaningful, Adaptive, Realistic and Time-bound*.[13] It may look like this: 'I will walk to the bridge after work (at 5:30 pm) on Tuesday and Thursday this week'. Two days are more achievable than saying you will do it every day. The bonus is you get a dose of the reward chemical, dopamine, for your achievement, which then provides some ongoing motivation. Visual reminders also help. Mark it off on the calendar. Detail your plan and mark your successes. It also helps to have a Plan B such as: 'If it is raining, I will use an online walk-at-home program.'

You can focus on one of the many activities that fit your chosen value. 'Growth' may be about learning a new skill such as yoga, drawing or photography; 'Connection' may be fishing with a friend or eating out with your family. The possibilities are endless.

Possible self-care activities

Painting	Craft	Tai Chi
Walking	Fishing	Gardening
Being on Country	Yoga	Boating
Enjoying nature	Camping	Yarning
Drawing	Mindfulness	Photography
Running	Being with friends	Journalling
Going to the beach	Eating out	Watch a movie
Competitive sport	Swimming	Read a book
Hiking	Family time	Play a sport
Weaving	Helping someone	Go for a massage
Going to a sporting event	Go to a spiritual place	Having a picnic

Sometimes, self-care may only require us to take a breath and notice what we are already doing rather than doing an additional activity. You may already be gardening each weekend but look at it as a chore. However, on reflection, you may realise that you enjoy this time in nature, the physical exertion and the sense of achievement. Perhaps you have opportunities to yarn with friends or colleagues but are usually in a rush to do the next thing. By noticing that you value their friendship and practising being present, you can add value to these activities and enjoy the connection they offer. Often finding what makes the sun shine for us is reconnecting with and being grateful for what we are already doing.

When more than self-care is needed

Teaching can be very stressful, impacting people's wellbeing significantly, so a little mental health advice is needed. The workload is high, and responsibilities to students, parents and the various levels of the education system can be overwhelming. Sometimes work conflicts with our values and needs. Current research shows that although teachers value collegial support, this is often unavailable as their colleagues are experiencing struggles themselves.[14] While self-care is a good place to start, it is not an elixir for everything. Seeking professional help when needed is essential; the trick is recognising when it is required. When we are in a bad place, we are not good at judging this, so listen to your family and friends; they know when you are not your usual self. Seeking help could mean making an appointment with a counsellor or a psychologist.

One of the better things COVID has left us with is more flexibility in how we can 'see' people, with telehealth being far more established. Many psychologists offer appointments by Skype or other platforms, which can make it easier to fit them into busy family and work schedules. Some people like these, some do not, but it is finding what works for you. Another option is talking to your doctor initially and, if necessary, getting a referral to see a mental health professional. Seeing a psychologist (in Australia) is cheaper if you have a Mental Health Plan from the GP.

The name 'mental health plan' sometimes puts people off as they link it with mental illness. However, I believe we all need a plan of how to maintain or regain our wellbeing, whether a doctor aids it or whether it is our personal goal for physical and mental health. A plan helps us stay on track. So do not get put off by the name. It is part of a holistic health plan. Another alternative is contacting your workplace's Employee Assistance Program (EAP). It is confidential and free. Finally, there are organisations such as Lifeline and Beyond Blue, which have a range of resources and ways of interacting, such as by text, phone and web chat. Remember, 'It is okay not to be okay', but you do not need to stay there. Help is available.

Self-care will help you stay anchored in the storm – and staying anchored is essential to maintaining your and your student's wellbeing and safety. You are the captain, and if you get swept away, there is little hope for the crew. People often protest that they do not have the time to indulge in self-care and wonder how it relates to supporting students' emotional regulation. You want to manage *their* regulation, right? Yes, this is true. However, to do this effectively, you not only need to model self-regulation, but you also need to assist the students with co-regulation. It takes many experiences of co-regulation before a child can self-regulate, and you need sufficient resilience to stay calm and connected while they learn this skill.

Many of us come from an era where we felt we needed to be productive at all times. The world has changed, and what is required to survive and thrive is very different. We need a new definition of productive. Many people are experiencing increased anxiety, and that is partly attributed to us attempting to do *'today's jobs with yesterday's tools'*.[15] Self-care *is* productive. It increases your overall sense of wellbeing. If you are chronically struggling, this can appear as physical and mental health issues. It can impact a student's learning and damage relationships. Dissatisfaction or disillusionment with your work may result. Most children are excellent at picking up on your vibes; their behaviour may reflect and amplify your feelings. Parents know this only too well. When they are having a bad day, their children will press all their buttons – even ones they did not know were there. This observation is valuable, and later in the book, we will explore how this can be turned around and used as a strategy for understanding how a child is feeling.

Sonya had a chronic shortage of time already and did not feel she could take on anything new; however, she also had enough insight to know that if she did nothing, nothing would improve. She decided to try doing some short 'get the wriggles out' activities with her class each day and to go for a brisk walk with her son and her dog two afternoons a week (once during the school week and once on the weekend). To ensure her goal was realistic and achievable, Sonya decided not to focus on diet and sleep at the moment, just to increase her exercise. However, the type of exercise she chose was consistent with her goal of improving her connection with her son and her students. It also increased her time spent outdoors in nature, which had been lacking in her life. She found that her son and dog looked forward to this time. They explored different routes, sometimes having serious discussions, sometimes laughing together, and sometimes silently enjoying one another's company. Initially, it felt like a chore, another demand on her time. However, after a while, Sonya started to look forward to this time. Other things began to fall into place without her even noticing at first. They ate healthier foods, and her sleep improved, making everything else less of a struggle. This example may sound like an unachievable fairy tale. However, the evidence shows that even a single occasion of aerobic exercise can improve our mood and decrease stress levels and even improve our cognitive functioning.[16]

'Self-care is giving the world the best of you instead of what is left of you.'[17]

Your challenge, should you choose to accept it, is ...

1. Choose one self-care activity to focus on – exercise, sleep, diet – or something that makes the sun shine for you. Ideally, choose something that also fits with your values and takes you toward the life you want to live.

2. Establish a SMART goal. I will (do this activity) on (which days) at (what time) this week. If I cannot do it because of weather or unexpected events, I will (alternate plan).

3. Put a visual reminder on the fridge and mark successes on the calendar.

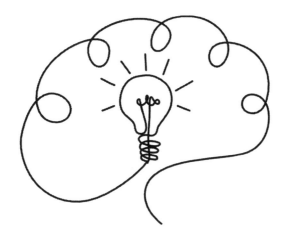

CHAPTER 2

NAVIGATION SYSTEMS

*F*rank (Teacher, Year 1)*: Why can't Charli stay at her desk and follow instructions? It was a simple task: copy a few words from the board into her book. Nothing too challenging. Within 30 seconds, she wanders around the class, disturbing others who are working. When told to return to her desk, she sat for a minute and even picked up her pencil. I thought, 'Success!' And then she was off again. This behaviour happens every day. She knows the rules. I have talked to her, spoken to her mum, tried changing whom she is sitting near, and attempted to sit her right away from the others. I have even tried threatening her with consequences. Nothing works.*

When a teacher's exasperation collides with the child's increasing frustration due to being developmentally unable to comply, the potential for a storm is high. Matching expectations, learning content and teaching methods with the child's brain development is an everyday challenge, particularly in prep and lower primary school. This planning is difficult to navigate as age-appropriateness may not correspond to developmental appropriateness. There are many developmental variations to consider: those that fall within the broad range of typical development, those with global developmental delays, and those with delays in specific areas. Whether typical or not, brain development is an ongoing process relevant to teachers at all levels of the education system. This chapter will focus on the range of typical brain development – when navigation systems are standard. The next chapter will look at neurodiversity and when brain systems work differently.

In the scenario at the beginning of this chapter, it would be easy for Charli to be considered disobedient and non-compliant. However, a better understanding of neurodevelopment would make us curious why she may behave this way. Curiosity would reduce frustration for the teacher and enable a problem-solving approach. The missing skills would be acknowledged and scaffolded, producing a learning outcome. The child would feel safe and connected in the classroom, enabling them to learn most effectively.

Understanding the typical neurodevelopment of children allows us to recognise when things are not typical. Teachers are well-placed to notice patterns of behaviour that do not fit the usual challenges of students of a particular chronological age. However, even in targeted early childhood education programs, teachers do not feel confident in their knowledge of childhood development theories and their links to practice.[18] This is even more evident for teachers of higher-level classes where the study of brain development and the implications for learning and teaching appears to have been a significant gap in their course of study. Fortunately, some current teacher education programs appear to be addressing this gap; however, it will take a long time for this knowledge to be generalised.

Without knowledge of brain development, people often attribute a student's behaviour to their character. Students are assumed to have actively decided to behave this way. With this assumption in mind, some teachers and parents firmly believe that behavioural consequences, such as time out, are the most effective way to achieve behavioural change. However, this approach can increase frustration for both the teacher and the child as it does not teach the skills the child needs to learn or meet the needs the child is communicating. It often leads to significant upset for the child, prolonging their disengagement from learning as the child then hides under the desk trying to manage their emotions. It may also make the teacher feel ineffectual and erode their confidence as they interpret the behaviour as a personal affront. Storms will proliferate. If this is the child's early schooling experience, it will not promote the joy of learning. If school processes inadvertently trigger the fight, flight or freeze responses repeatedly in a child, the child's nervous system will be on alert continuously. It will not take much to push them outside their 'window of tolerance',[19] and they will dysregulate easily. This consideration does not mean there are no boundaries to behaviour or reasonable expectations; it is about what is reasonable to expect given the stage of development.

Ideally, a teacher supports students in gaining the skills to manage these behaviours but accepts that time will also be a significant factor. Alongside these challenging behaviours, the child is also developing many skills and strengths. Noticing and acknowledging these will help build a positive relationship with the student, allowing them to be more open to learning and developing the necessary skills.

Expecting a child to do something they cannot do because of their stage of development also has social justice implications. Navigating expectations around this with knowledge and curiosity is much easier. When a child develops new skills, the pathway to attaining them is not a straight line. Just because they could do it yesterday does not mean they can do it today. Hunger, tiredness, stress, trauma or sensory overwhelm can significantly reduce their capacity. It is always helpful to remember that the student did not wake up this morning and think, *'I will make the lives of those around me hard today'*. Approaching the behaviour with curiosity and compassion will produce the best learning and emotional wellbeing outcomes for the student.

In the example above, consideration from a developmental point of view may be: is Charli 'able' to do this? Are her executive functions sufficiently developed to maintain attention and focus and overcome impulsivity? Executive functions include attentional control, working memory, inhibition and problem-solving. They allow us to plan, organise and prioritise, stay focused on a task until completion, understand different points of view, regulate impulses, and keep track of our actions.

Executive functions start developing early in life but continue developing into the mid-twenties or even to age thirty. From a position of curiosity, are Charli's executive functions sufficiently developed to comply with your request? Can she remember what is on the board long enough to write it on the paper? Can she organise starting the task effectively? Can she overcome the natural impulse for a six-year-old to move and interact with others?

And then there are functional considerations to be curious about:

- Can she see the writing on the board, and can she 'track' it?
- Can she hold the pencil effectively, or is that difficult for her?
- Does she have difficulty sitting? Does she have weak core muscles, pain or fatigue?
- From a cognitive perspective, do the letters' groupings or the letters themselves mean anything to her — or are they just random shapes?
- Is she able to hear and process your instructions?

If behaviour is viewed with curiosity about what it is communicating, it increases compassion. It also decreases the frustration of both students and teachers and reduces the potential for storms in the classroom.

Some challenging behaviours are developmentally appropriate even when they are pretty exasperating. It is normal and okay for us to get frustrated sometimes. There is no such thing as a perfect parent or teacher, and a perfect parent or teacher is not what the child needs. A child needs an adult who can self-regulate most of the time and repair relationships when needed. The ability to repair relationships is essential for the rest of their lives, and they depend on us to model this skill.

> 'Understanding child development takes the emphasis away from the child's character – looking at the child as good or bad. If the emphasis is put on behaviour as communication, the child is then helped to learn a more acceptable manner of communication.'[20]

Brain development

Brain development commences in utero; anything that affects the mum can impact the growing baby. Chronic maternal stress, such as that caused by living in a domestic violence situation, a lack of adequate nutrition, and the use of tobacco, alcohol or other drugs, can all impact healthy brain development. There are stages of development where the brain is particularly susceptible; however, all of these factors interact in complex ways, making it impossible to predict the harm caused by these factors in combination or isolation. Prevention is key. For a baby to have the best opportunity for developing into a strong and healthy child, the mum must be safe, have good antenatal care, have access to adequate nutrition, and be supported in her efforts not to drink, smoke or take drugs. The best support those surrounding them can offer is to abstain from substance use and engage in a healthy and respectful lifestyle.

After they are born, the baby's brain continues to be shaped by the experiences to which they are exposed. Strong connections with caregivers in a safe and predictable environment are essential for the baby's brain to develop in the best way possible.[21] According to Lou Cozolino (2012), the author of *Social Neuroscience of Education*:

> *'Optimal sculpting of key neural networks through healthy early relationships allows us to think well of ourselves, trust others, regulate our emotions, maintain positive expectations, and utilise our intellectual and emotional intelligence in moment-to-moment decision-making.'* [22] (14)

The absence of an attentive and attuned caregiver who consistently meets the infant's needs can have lifelong consequences. While the brain is 'plastic' and can make new connections throughout life, the brain's lower regions (the brain stem, midbrain and limbic system) are the hardest to heal or change after their initial development.[21,23] The upper regions of the brain are more responsive to intervention.

A child's brain is 90% of its adult size by the time they are four years old.[21] The extent of brain development during this time is one of the reasons why the first few years are so important. Ideal development in each brain area depends on exposure to specific experiences at specific times.[21]

All models of brain development and nervous system function are very simplified and provide a way of understanding what is happening rather than being scientifically accurate. Brains are incredibly complex, with many areas of the brain involved in any particular process and multiple areas of the brain establishing connections and growing at any one time. However, with this caveat, a child's brain develops from the bottom up and side to side, with the brain stem being the first region to develop.[24] The age shown for development is when the most significant development in each area occurs, although it starts before and continues after these cut-off times. During these critical times, adverse experiences will have the most impact. There are many reasons for differences in brain development, including neurodiversity and trauma. Adverse childhood experiences may cause lifetime disadvantages, which are entirely preventable. Becoming more aware of child development needs and risk factors can motivate us to advocate for education, prevention and healing in our communities.

I have referred to the person/persons caring for the baby simply as their carers. I have not referred to them as primary carers in recognition of different cultural perspectives on the care of children. Many aunts, uncles, nannas and pops may be intimately involved in their care, as well as Mum and Dad.

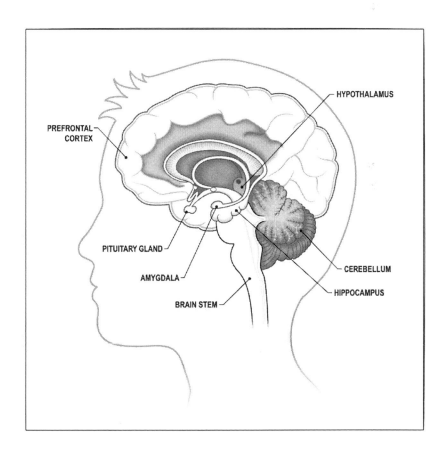

Brain stem

The brain stem is located at the base of the brain and connects the brain and the spinal cord. The most active growth for the brain stem is between zero and nine months.[21] The brain stem is responsible for basic survival, controlling our breathing, heart rate, swallowing and body temperature.[21] It plays an essential role in attention, arousal and consciousness. It is a motor and sensory information pathway and is also associated with our survival modes: fight, flight, freeze or collapse.

For optimal development, the baby must trust that an attentive caregiver will consistently meet their physical and safety needs. A baby instinctively uses strategies to engage a caregiver by cooing and waving their arms, reacting to the caregivers' interactions, smiling and being cute. Looking at this quite cynically, these actions are all designed to suck the carer in – to ensure that they will meet their needs and protect them. When we respond to their cries and do our best to figure out what they want, the baby learns that the world is a safe place with people who will love and protect them, and respond to their physical, emotional, social and growth needs.

The baby may experience toxic stress if these needs are repeatedly unmet. Some babies may persist in crying to get a caregiver to meet their physical or emotional needs; others may initially cry but eventually give up and become quiet and withdrawn as they learn their first strategy does not work. These adaptations they have learnt to aid their survival may replay in the classroom, even though they are inappropriate in this context.

There are many possibilities as to why a child's needs were not met, and it is essential not to be judgemental of the parents. The child may have had chronically neglected needs because their carer suffered from depression or another mental illness, or because the child was so ill that medical intervention to ensure their survival was prioritised over emotional needs. The infant's carer may have had a physical illness or chronic disability that limited their ability to respond. They may have been overwhelmed with life, utterly exhausted and unable to meet the baby's needs. Alternatively, they may have had an alcohol or drug problem, and the nature of these addictions means they prioritised these needs over all else. Blame does not help the child and the family move forward and do the hard work necessary to heal this damage. The parents may have also had a tough childhood, compromising their ability to respond to the infant. Dr Bruce Perry (2021) tells us that we must consider 'what happened to you' when looking at child or adult behaviour.

> *'We have talked a lot about how the actions of caregivers influence the child, but it's important to remember that those caregivers were also children influenced by their caregivers. The effects of trauma stretch far and wide across generations and across communities, and it's important to always come back to our central question with compassion: What happened to you?'* [25]

Diencephalon and cerebellum

The cerebellum is located just above the brain stem and toward the back of the brain. Between the brain stem and the cortex is the diencephalon.

The most active growth period for the diencephalon and the cerebellum is from six months to two years.[21] The cerebellum is responsible for balance and coordination and involves voluntary motor movement, muscle tone and equilibrium. The diencephalon is vital in relaying and processing sensory and motor information and has a role in managing emotions. At this stage of brain development, promoting a feeling of safety and connection and providing a range of experiences that use all the senses is crucial.[21] Physical activity is also essential to aid the development of this part of the brain.[21] If a child is left in its cot, it has little stimulation, which would then affect the development of this part of the brain.

Our senses are much more than the five senses we generally consider: hearing, sight, smell, touch and taste. Some other senses are proprioception, interoception and the vestibular system. The *vestibular system* allows us to coordinate balance and movement. Children with processing challenges related to the vestibular system may be sensitive to, seek out, or be slower to respond to vestibular input. Those *sensitive* to vestibular input may avoid using swings and climbing on the playground equipment; those *seeking* vestibular input may be unable to sit still or persist in rocking their chair, a common issue in classrooms. A child with difficulty processing vestibular input may quickly lose balance and appear clumsy.

Proprioception allows us to know where we are in space. A child with trouble processing proprioceptive stimuli may have poor body awareness and motor planning, poor postural control, and sensory-seeking behaviours. Some examples of what this may look like include: pressing so hard on their pencil that the lead breaks, having difficulties walking up and down stairs, slumping and often moving in their chair, difficulty balancing on one foot, and chewing their clothes or other non-food items.

Interoception is the sense that lets you feel and understand what is going on inside your body – that you are hungry, that your heart is beating fast, or that your muscles are tense. This sense is involved in self-regulation. People with anger management issues, who report going from '0 to 100' without noticing, often have trouble feeling what is happening in their bodies. If a child has problems processing these senses, an occupational therapist is the best person to assist.

Limbic system

The limbic system includes the hippocampus, the amygdala and the hypothalamus. It is deep in the brain, above the brainstem and below the cerebral cortex.

The most active growth of the limbic system occurs between one year and four years.[21] The limbic system is responsible for our emotional responses, behavioural regulation and connection to others. Our initial connection is to our caregivers. Also associated with the limbic system are attachment, social language development, empathy, tolerance and interpretation of non-verbal language. Positive, safe experiences during this time provide a foundation for future relationships.[21,23] While each area of the brain has some involvement with emotional regulation, the limbic system is particularly important.

Cortex

The cerebral cortex is the outer layer of the brain.

The cortex's most active growth period is between three and six years.[21] It is responsible for thinking, reasoning and creativity. Essential skills such as paying attention, making decisions and planning are part of the cortex's function. The cortex is also where we process social and emotional information. This part of the brain continues to develop into the mid-twenties; however, it remains able to grow and change throughout life, enabling us to learn new skills and ways of thinking.[21] Healthy development of the cortex depends on the healthy development of the brain's lower regions and ongoing safety and connection.

Returning to Charli's story

Children with emotional regulation difficulties are assessed against typical developmental milestones when referred to specialist services. Just as children have average times for physical development, such as taking their first steps, there are also average times for learning to manage big emotions and for their cognitive, social and moral development. To complicate matters, even with everything else being equal, development is not in a straight line. For example, Charli appeared eager to please adults at five years old, generally doing as she was asked and presenting as a charming young child. Shortly after she turned five and a half though, family and friends wondered what had happened to their well-behaved and agreeable little person. She became less compliant, challenged adults about their decisions and directions, and argued with her peers. Only some of the time, but often enough to cause frustration. Toward the end of the year, Charli started to appear restless and had difficulty sitting still for any length of time, which caused some concern.

Now Charli is nearly six years old and has started school. The new environment and increased expectations have exacerbated both the behaviours and the frustration. Most of Charli's behaviours could be explained by typical developmental challenges and her still-developing executive skills, such as task initiation and impulse control. However, we must also remain alert for other causes, such as trauma, developmental delays, neurodiversity and physical issues. Remain curious and compassionate. What else have you observed? The critical thing to remember is that this is not a character flaw or a 'difficult child'. It is about the brain and its development. That is not to say you are powerless in this process. You can help shape that development by modelling and guiding acceptable behaviours and remembering that learning does not occur when nervous systems are in the fight, flight or freeze mode. Learning happens when the child feels 'safe and social'. You can teach and reinforce the skills needed for success in school.

By the time Charli is six and a half years old, she will be more easygoing, get along better with adults and peers, and enjoy learning new things and then sharing them with others.[26] In my work, I often see children around this age go from learning being a struggle and constantly being in trouble and dysregulating, to wanting to teach me and my friend Boris (a bear puppet) what they have learnt. Until this point, learning through play will likely provide the most favourable outcomes, socially, emotionally and cognitively.[27] Unfortunately, some have gained a reputation that disadvantages them by that time.

Play – how children learn

Providing access to play is one of the most powerful things we can do to aid children's brain development. Over the years, the time spent playing has decreased, and the types of play have changed. Many children are more likely to be using screens of one sort or another rather than being outside enjoying unstructured and adventurous play. We are afraid they may hurt themselves, or bad people may be around. Without the opportunity to take some risks, children have become more anxious about taking them, including the risks they need to take in learning: the risk of being wrong. Many children have both parents working, limiting the time and energy available for taking children to the park or on adventures. To compound this, early years education emphasises learning according to a curriculum – learning through play in some cases – but generally, children are exposed earlier to structured learning rather than learning through unstructured play. It is through play with their peers that children learn social skills, problem-solving, conflict resolution and emotional regulation.[28,29]

Through play, they can process their emotions and inevitable life events. When playing, children enter a world of imagination where they learn to build a narrative and communicate that to another. They learn how far they can push one another and practise nurturing and protective roles. In play, children exceed their everyday behaviour and demonstrate skills that are still developing in other contexts.[30]

While providing (or not providing) access to play in the early years is predominantly a systems issue, it is worth being aware of how the push to 'educate' earlier impacts a child's developing brain. While I know this statement will not resonate well with educators who have limited options for consequences for students not doing their work, not allowing a child to play as a consequence of not being able to sit still and do their work is not likely to achieve the desired outcome. If a child cannot sit still, the antidote is running around, not confinement.

Play and physical exercise will likely make the child more amenable to working in the next session. Preventing play may produce internal or external emotional storms. Remain curious about why they cannot sit still and notice any patterns. They may be just having a bad day and can usually do what is required. We all have bad days and hope people will give us grace on those days. Alternatively, they may not yet have the skills, or something may have upset their world.

Charli and her teacher have made it through the challenges of her chronological age. It is not all good news for the classroom, however. Charli will likely be very talkative and may be extremely sensitive to criticism at six and a half years old.[26] This sensitivity can lead to upsets following the slightest correction. I certainly recognise the difficulty of having children at many stages of development within your classroom and the challenge of supporting each in their educational journey. Awareness of childhood development will help prevent frustration and allow you to focus more on skill development than behaviour management.

Saxon's story: *Further up the developmental ladder is twelve-year-old Saxon, who is struggling to focus and stay awake in class. Saxon is often late for the morning lessons and practically falls asleep after lunch. They are often moody and impulsive. It is frustrating. We know Saxon can do better.*

Does Saxon need to get their act together and go to sleep earlier? Or is this also a part of normal development? As always, be curious and compassionate, as there may be other factors. However, adolescents' circadian rhythm changes and their biology makes it difficult for them to go to sleep early and get up early. Verma, Yadav, Rani and Malik (2021) went so far as to say that adolescents' biological clock versus the expectations of society presents significant health concerns for young people due to chronic sleep deprivation.[31]

Compounding this is their still-developing executive function. While their ability to control impulses and focus (if not overtired) has improved, these functions will not fully develop until their mid-twenties.

A referral is always warranted to assess or monitor the child whenever parents or teachers are concerned. Parents and teachers have incredible insight and understanding of the child, so their concerns must be taken seriously. The most helpful book I have found that details normal development and when to seek help is by Dee Ray (2016), *A Therapist's Guide to Child Development: The Extraordinarily Normal Years.*[26] An appendix gives a brief but detailed outline of cognitive, social, emotional and moral development from three to twelve years. This book contains essential knowledge for teachers as well as therapists.

This chapter has looked only at 'normal' or typical development. As you have seen, even within this limited range, many children struggle to do what we expect just because their brains are not yet sufficiently developed. Things we see as simple tasks, such as sitting still, lining up, and being quiet, may be too complex and still need practice and guidance. Their failure to do as you ask may be labelled non-compliant and difficult. Without sufficient positive attention when they are learning to do the 'right' thing, the negative attention they get due to their behaviour may set them up to continue this behaviour even when they are developmentally able to comply. I have known children who have internalised that they are 'bad' and felt that everyone was against them at five years old because they were always in trouble for being unable to remain seated and do their work. It is heartbreaking to hear them say this or portray it in a sand tray, and even more so when we know there was no way they could comply at that stage of their developmental journey. This harsh self-concept is difficult to change, as is their reputation within the school.

On the other hand, some children who are beginning to develop the necessary executive skills work so hard at complying and being 'good' that they eventually break down in tears – or explode – as they become tired and overwhelmed. Doing the right thing can take much energy.

For these students, it sometimes appears that their meltdown has come out of nowhere, as their behaviour has been impeccable until that point. Sometimes children can maintain 'being good' until they get home, and then all hell breaks loose for their parents and siblings. Stuart Shanker, a leading expert in the theory of self-regulation, advises:

> *'For some children, just trying to sit still or inhibit an impulse takes an enormous amount of energy and there may not be enough left to sustain attention.'* [32]

Movement breaks and regulation activities can be helpful in both cases. We will look at these in further chapters.

Teachers already have much on their plate, and learning more about neurodevelopment may seem overwhelming. However, there are many benefits. Without this knowledge, you may feel like you are banging your head against a brick wall – but with it, you can take down those walls and build bridges that support brain growth. From my research, I found that many teachers felt their prime (and sometimes only) responsibility is teaching the curriculum. While the curriculum gives you the 'what' you should teach, understanding neurodevelopment gives you the 'how'. One without the other places everyone at a disadvantage. I believe that as time goes on, neurodevelopment will be essential knowledge for *all* teachers as brains keep developing throughout the school years. Knowledge can help prevent emotional storms and protect the wellbeing of the class.

In the next chapter, we will look at neurodiversity.

Your challenge, should you choose to accept it, is ...

1. Research the typical physical, moral, emotional and cognitive development for the age range in your class.

2. Research the normal developmental challenges.

3. Be curious. Reflect on one student who has problems with regulation. Consider whether it fits with the typical developmental challenges for that particular age. Or are there other possible explanations for the behaviour?

CHAPTER 3

ALTERNATIVE SYSTEMS

Jo's story (Teacher, Year 5): *The principal has told me that I have Sam in my class this year and that she has recently been diagnosed with autism spectrum disorder – level two. What does this even mean? Does she have learning difficulties? Behavioural problems? What support will she need? I saw a child with autism in my previous school, and they could not even stay in the classroom – and when they did, they disrupted all the other kids with their meltdowns and behaviours. What training will I get so I can support her? I have no experience in this. I am all for inclusivity, but how am I supposed to cater to this child and all the other kids without knowing anything about neurodiversity?*

Our world and systems are designed for the dominant version of typical people: typical height, typical ability, typical ways of learning – and typical brain structures. While society is slowly acknowledging, challenging and changing this situation, this is the reality that the non-dominant sections of the community face daily. While this chapter focuses on neurodiversity, we also need to consider that young people from other minority groups, such as those with physical disabilities, LGBTQIA+ students, migrants, refugees and Indigenous young people, also do not fit the dominant culture. Children from these groups may have different social needs and legitimate ways of learning that do not align with the education system. Advocates and educators must promote and provide equal access to education to those who do not fit the dominant mould, and knowledge is needed to do that. It can also take courage to contest the status quo and advocate for these students.

Understanding the needs and challenges of children and young people who navigate the world differently allows teachers to work with them rather than inadvertently against them. Additional knowledge of neurodiversity can help prevent student frustration and consequent dysregulation. Being aware of any disability and what that means for their functioning will help build an understanding of the enormous effort it can take to operate in a neurotypical world, and the costs it may have to their physical and mental health. Each student with a diagnosis is unique, with different abilities and strengths. This knowledge and understanding will assist you in providing the best educational opportunities for each child. Increased knowledge of disorders and disabilities will also help you to have the confidence to work with the other members of the child's support network. Again, curiosity and compassion are the keys.

Researchers estimate that 1 in 5 children and adults in the United States have learning and attention issues.[33] Alongside this finding, a survey of 1350 teachers from Kindergarten to Year 12 revealed that while the majority were highly interested in learning how to reach struggling learners, only 17% felt *'very prepared'* to teach children with mild to moderate learning difficulties.[34] This alarming fact aligns with a study in Australia where teachers felt ill-prepared for inclusive education.[35] The teachers identified that many systemic changes would be necessary to support its success. However, the number one request was professional development concerning various disabilities.[35] This aligns with research by Wray et al. (2022), which identified teacher education and professional development among the five components leading to teachers having the confidence needed to teach in inclusive classrooms.[36]

A lack of knowledge sets teachers and students up to struggle. A common issue is not understanding a child's need for fidgets or time out of the classroom. When a teacher denies a student access to the sensory input they need to focus and learn or denies the student breaks that would prevent dysregulation, it is like taking away the crutches of a child with a broken leg and expecting them to fully participate in school activities. This insensitivity is not intentional. However, efforts to be fair and consistent and have the same rules and consequences apply to all students can create inequitable access to education and increase frustration and disengagement. This approach may lead to emotional storms in the classroom. If teachers do not have a good understanding of the need that these accommodations fulfil, they may think that those suggesting them are rewarding 'bad' behaviour rather than assisting with regulation strategies.

Disorder or diversity

There is a strong movement toward changing how some disorders are considered, especially by people affected by them. Disorders such as attention deficit hyperactivity disorder (ADHD) and autism spectrum disorder (ASD) are increasingly described as neurodiversity, with the recognition that for many people, much of the disability experienced is a result of living in and trying to meet the expectations of a neurotypical world. There is extensive use of the medical model for diagnosing and treating these disorders, so it is worth considering both aspects of this, knowing that for many people, the most helpful response is to listen to how they define it, and their definition may lie somewhere in the middle. Currently, the medical model's diagnosis helps justify the additional support needed in the classroom. However, this is gradually changing to functional and needs assessments for disability support in the community and an evaluation of learning and support needs in the classroom.

With either understanding, accommodations may be needed to cater for the child's way of learning and their other needs. Sometimes students have sensory needs or processing difficulties. Catering for these is part of providing an equal opportunity for education. Withholding what they need to regulate contributes to meltdowns and educational disadvantages and can also contribute to lifelong mental health issues. At the time of writing this book, the Disability Royal Commission was hearing evidence in response to an issues paper identifying that the needs of students with disabilities were not being met in the education system, demonstrating the seriousness of this issue.[37]

Many strategies that assist children with ADHD or ASD are also helpful for those with FASD or trauma. Many diagnoses have overlapping symptoms, and a child may have multiple diagnoses. Each child, with or without a diagnosis, is unique and individual needs may vary. However, there are whole-of-class strategies that will benefit all students and help maintain calm in the classroom. Additional support must be provided with sensitivity. Children with diverse needs have identified that a teacher singling them out causes additional stress. This issue can be overcome by having pre-arranged plans (e.g. somewhere they can go if they need to leave the classroom, a signal to indicate the need to go, or pre-arranged break times to 'go and get a drink', so they can go without needing to ask permission).

While planning to minimise the storm's impact is good, planning for prevention is much better.

Autism spectrum disorder

In 2018, Autism Spectrum Australia (Aspect) estimated the prevalence of autism in Australia to be 1 in 70.[38] Autism is a lifelong developmental condition that affects, among other things, the way an individual relates to their environment and the way they interact with other people. Children with autism often receive a diagnosis before they start school. However, at other times, social, behavioural and regulation issues in the classroom will prompt investigation. Others are not diagnosed until they are adults and feel a sense of relief when there is an explanation for their struggles. It affects more boys than girls, and there can be more delays in getting a diagnosis for girls. Anxiety is a common problem for children with autism.

According to the *Diagnostic and Statistical Manual 5th ed* (2013), the diagnostic criteria for autism spectrum disorder are:

- *Persistent deficits in social communication and social interaction across multiple contexts*
- *Restricted, repetitive patterns of behaviour, interests or activities*
- *Symptoms must be present in the early developmental period; however, these may not be evident until social demands exceed the child's limited capacities, or they may be masked by learned strategies in later life*
- *Symptoms cause clinically significant impairment in social, occupational or other important areas of current functioning.* [39]
  (50)

The level of support required depends on where on the spectrum the child sits. It is important to remember that each child is different, and their blend of difficulties and strengths will be unique.

Level One – Requires support
- May have difficulties with communicating and social interactions
- May not read body language and social cues successfully
- May have difficulty organising themselves and their possessions and struggle with change and transitions.[39(52)]

Level Two – Requires substantial support
- Similar issues to level one – but more significant difficulties
- May have narrow interests and repetitive behaviours.[39(52)]

Level Three – Requires very substantial support
- Severe difficulties in verbal and non-verbal communication
- Extreme versions of difficulties in levels one and two
- Repetitive behaviours.[39(52)]

There have been significant increases in the number of people diagnosed with autism over recent years; however, research indicates that this represents improved diagnostic methods and classifications rather than more people who are autistic.[38] There is an argument about whether we should use person-first or identity-first language, i.e. a person with autism or an autistic person. Again, listening to the person is essential. For many, being autistic is part of their identity, particularly as they get older and find 'their people'. For others, it remains a disability that causes significant impairments.

The results of the Survey of Disability, Ageing and Carers (2018) will aid the understanding of the impact of ASD on students. This survey found that 77.7% of people with autism aged five to twenty years who attended an education facility faced difficulties that affected their education.[40] The most frequently identified issues were fitting in socially, learning difficulties and difficulties with communication.[40] Almost half of the young people identified they required more educational support than they received.[40] Considering this lack of support alongside the finding that 31.2% of people without autism have a bachelor's degree or higher, while only 8.1% of people with autism achieve this level of education, you can see how the lack of support translates into a disparity of lifetime opportunities.[40] While some people with autism also have a cognitive impairment, many do not – and may have exceptional knowledge and abilities.

Returning to Jo's story (ASD)

Jo is right. She needs more knowledge to support Sam in her class. Hopefully, she could successfully seek assistance from her school to access professional development, which would improve her confidence. If not, it would benefit her wellbeing and her entire class if she pursued this for herself. Great online courses and free resources focusing on teaching children with ASD are available from Sue Larkey (suelarkey. com.au). Much helpful information for teachers, parents and health workers is available from Dr Tony Attwood, the guru of autism and Dr Michelle Garnett (attwoodandgarnettevents.com). An insightful student's perspective is available from Summer Farrelly (summerfarrelly. com.au).

Jo would need to find out what additional teacher or teacher aide support was available from the school and whether the support person knows about ASD. If not, it would be helpful to do the training together. If Sam has an existing relationship with a support person, it may aid the transition if they can accompany her to the new class, even if it is only for the first week.

The next step would be to talk to Sam's previous teacher to find out not only about her struggles but also about her strengths and interests and the strategies the previous teacher had found helpful in supporting Sam. Did Sam use fidgets, was there an arrangement for taking a break, and where did it work best for her to sit? It is helpful to maintain as much consistency as possible during change. Sometimes conversations about a student can get stuck on the struggles, but it is essential that strengths also feature in this conversation. This discussion would answer Jo's questions about learning difficulties and behavioural problems. However, it is crucial to remember that the relationship developed will substantially impact behaviour, so what is evident in one class may be different in another. Sam's diagnosis says she is level two, meaning that although she will need substantial support within the classroom, Sam is not at the extreme end of the autism spectrum.

It would be ideal if Jo's first contact with Sam's parents was not when she was in trouble. Early contact with her parents would allow Jo to discover their hopes and dreams for Sam, what works for them, and their struggles at home. It is beneficial to know if sleep is an issue (and it often is for children with ASD and, therefore, for their families) as this will impact functioning at school, emotional regulation, and potentially the time they arrive at school after a sleepless night. It is also helpful to find out from the parents who else is part of the child's support team so that everyone can be on the same page. For example, the occupational therapist may suggest what sensory supports are required, when to use them, and the rules to put around their use.

Every child is different; however, these are some possible strengths of children with autism. Focusing on strengths rather than 'fixing' difficulties can give better results, improve relationships and demonstrate respect for difference. Using special interests and strengths will provide the best results where the student needs some skill development.

Autism Strengths [41, 42]	
Visual learning and thinking	Punctuality
Strong adherence to rules	Logical thinking
Knowledge about special interests	Rote memory ability
Reliable and honest	Precise and focused on detail
Thinking outside the box	A drive for perfection and order

While focusing on strengths, we must also acknowledge difficulties to alleviate these. These are *some* of the issues that *some* children with ASD struggle with and some suggestions.

- Simultaneously looking and listening may be challenging and should not be required.
- The child may understand what you say literally and struggle with idioms and metaphors. Abstract thinking may be difficult. It helps if you are clear, concise and concrete.
- The student may not generalise information well. 'You said not to climb that tree. I did not know you meant this one, too.' This may not be just a cheeky response.
- Many are visual learners. Verbal information may take longer to process and retain. Too much verbal input may create sensory overload, leading to meltdowns. Again, clear and concise works well, supported by visual information.
- Making choices can be difficult. It helps to give options but limit these and be specific.
- Some students with ASD enjoy verbal arguments. Short, calm redirections can prevent you from buying into them.
- People with ASD may also have sensory processing difficulties. If we do not meet sensory needs, it may lead to regulation and behavioural problems. A fidget, a wobble cushion, or a weighted lap toy or blanket may aid focus and attention and reduce anxiety. Normal classroom noises can be overwhelming. Noise-cancelling headphones can help.
- Sensory breaks are essential. Girls, in particular, may cope all day at school and then have significant meltdowns when they go home at the end of the day. Breaks, even when they don't seem necessary from a school perspective, can help avoid after-school meltdowns, relieving the pressure on the families.
- If the child struggles with writing or reading texts, text-to-speech and speech-to-text apps are helpful. These are readily available on mobile phones for social communication and within Microsoft Word for school work.

- A child with level three ASD may be non-verbal and have no concept of danger.

Attention deficit hyperactivity disorder

Researchers estimate that about 1 in 20 children in Australia have ADHD.[43] Therefore, it is likely that at least one child in each classroom will have this diagnosis, making some knowledge about this disorder essential. It is quite probable that there will be others with ADHD-like symptoms but not a diagnosis. More boys than girls are diagnosed with this disability.[43]

The medical model defines attention deficit hyperactivity disorder (ADHD) as a neurodevelopmental disorder and a mental health condition. According to the *Diagnostic and Statistical Manual 5th ed* (DSM-V), people with ADHD:

> '... *show a persistent pattern of inattention and/or hyperactivity and impulsivity that interferes with their functioning or development. For an ADHD diagnosis, six or more symptoms must be present within either the inattention or hyperactivity/ impulsivity section. They must be present for six or more months in two or more settings. There must be clear evidence that they interfere with their quality of life, learning or relationships.*'[39] [59]

A range of symptoms are listed in the *DSM-V* (2013), but they fit within these categories.

Inattention symptoms
- difficulty concentrating
- forgetting instructions
- moving from one task to another without completion.

Impulsivity
- talking over the top of others
- losing control of emotions easily
- being accident-prone
- acting without thinking.

Overactivity
- constant fidgeting and restlessness.[39 (59-60)]

Before and after a child is diagnosed with ADHD, their parents may face much judgement about their parenting style; however, ADHD is not a result of bad parenting. Nonetheless, specific parenting and teaching practices can be helpful. Parents can also face judgement over their decision to medicate or not to medicate once their child has received an ADHD diagnosis.[44] There is medical support for and against medication, so it is necessary to understand parents' difficulties with this decision. Medicating a child is a serious issue with potential long-term health and wellbeing impacts. It is a tough judgement call.

Sometimes, while the parents may be aware of the child's difficulties, the extent of the issues at school is not evident at home. If the child spends much active time outside and the parents have learnt to work with their difficulties, they may not see the child's problems in the classroom. Understanding this from both sides may require some parent/teacher meetings, not just about the behaviour in the school, but finding the exceptions because it is in these exceptions that there may be strategies that will work. ADHD appears to have a strong genetic factor,[45] so Mum or Dad may have an intimate understanding of what the child is experiencing, even if they do not have a diagnosis. This insight may aid their understanding of what is helpful for the child, which the parents may already provide at home, not in a planned way, but instinctively.

Medication should not be considered an alternative to appropriate accommodations in the classroom. This approach would be like prescribing a child some painkillers rather than providing physio for a physical complaint. It may provide a 'quick fix' but may also be harmful to the child. A trial of strategies should always be the first step. Parent education and the implementation of appropriate accommodations in the classroom are essential, even when the child is medicated. Remember that things that may be easy for other students, like sitting at their desks, putting their hand up before speaking, and waiting their turn, may take a great deal of effort for these students.

Brian's story (ADHD)

Brian is a six-year-old boy with a recent diagnosis of ADHD. He cannot stay still in class and annoys and distracts everyone else. The teachers are concerned that his inability to focus (except when he is using the computer, iPad or playing Lego) affects his ability to learn and negatively affects the rest of the class. These times when Brian is hyper-focused are often cited as 'he can focus if he wants to'. He never finishes his work, so he often misses fun activities, such as movement and music breaks, action games, and even playtime at recess. It is hard to find a consequence that will motivate him to do what he needs to do. Brian will dysregulate and run from the room if pushed to do things. His behaviour is affecting his relationships with both peers and adults. The paediatrician has not yet prescribed medication and has asked us to try accommodations within the classroom. What can we do that we are not already doing?

You may be doing all you can. It would be worth documenting the strategies you are currently using and their success or otherwise, as this can be helpful feedback for the paediatrician when they review the child. From the information provided, the first step would be to prioritise his engagement in movement and physical activities in the classroom and the playground. The current consequences are likely to worsen the situation rather than improve it. You may find that after he has done a movement activity, he may be able to focus for a short while. These observations are valuable.

Some other ideas to consider:

- Establish a strong relationship. Knowing the student's interests and strengths will help achieve this.
- As with ASD, build on their strengths.
- Try to limit distractions through the seating organisation.
- Have clear rules, consistent expectations and logical consequences.
- Visual reminders will benefit many students.
- Provide positive attention frequently. Look for opportunities as they may be hard to find initially. The aim is to meet attention/connection needs with positive attention so as not to re-enforce inappropriate behaviours.
- When correcting behaviour, be matter-of-fact and not emotional. Briefly correct inappropriate behaviour immediately. Be specific about what the student has done wrong and have clear consequences. Be aware of the symptoms of ADHD so you do not give consequences for something that may be out of their control.
- Ensure sensory and regulation needs are met. An occupational therapist can assist with determining these.

Consider how the difficulties a student with ADHD has in the classroom may be beneficial in another context. This is not to say they are not challenging or that some children do not need medication, but it is worth considering whether the necessary restrictions in the classroom are a contributing factor.

ADHD Strengths [47]	ADHD Difficulties
Energy – valuable in a work environment	Unable to sit still in the classroom
Adventurousness (willingness to take risks)	Risky behaviour
Looking at the big picture	Missing details
Creativity – thinking outside the box	Difficulty following instructions
Comfortable with change and chaos	Impulsivity
Hyperfocus on things that interest them	Lack of focus generally

Foetal alcohol spectrum disorder

Foetal alcohol spectrum disorder (FASD) is a neurodevelopmental disorder/prenatal brain injury caused by alcohol exposure in utero. This situation may arise because Mum was unaware that she was pregnant at the time or because Mum could not stop drinking because of addiction, social circumstances, or her experience of personal, collective or intergenerational trauma. FASD is a sensitive issue that does not receive the publicity it needs. Sometimes, even today, it occurs through a lack of education and understanding of the damage it can do.

While there is little data about the prevalence of FASD in Australia, a study in Fitzroy Crossing (Western Australia) found the prevalence to be extremely high at 19.4%.[48] Global data suggests that high levels of FASD are likely in communities with high social disadvantage and poverty levels. This rate amounts to 4 children in a class of 20 students if you work in a school in a remote, Indigenous community with high levels of historical and current trauma – and most will not have a diagnosis. Additionally, students with FASD may have families who endure the effects of intergenerational trauma, and their parents may also have FASD making it difficult for them to engage with the education system. The students may live in out-of-home care, have a trauma history, or live with trauma every day. Attachment issues may further complicate the student's behaviours and needs. Alternatively, the child may now have a safe, connected and stable home life but still suffer the consequences of an adverse start in life.

When children have FASD, the sentinel facial features may be evident, but in many cases, they are not. The sentinel facial features are:

- Small palpebral fissures (i.e. a short, horizontal length of the eye-opening)
- Smooth philtrum (i.e. diminished or absent ridges between the upper lip and nose)
- A thin upper lip.[49]

The stage of the foetus' development when alcohol exposure occurs, will determine which systems may be affected. The effect also depends on other factors, such as maternal health, age, nutrition, tobacco or other drug use, stress levels, or exposure to violence.

The *Australian Guide to the Diagnosis of Fetal Alcohol Spectrum Disorder* states that FASD may be diagnosed if there has been prenatal alcohol exposure *and* severe impairment in three or more domains.[49] Domains that may be affected are:

- Brain structure and neurology
- Motor skills
- Cognition
- Language
- Academic achievement
- Memory
- Attention
- Executive function, impulse control, hyperactivity

- Affect regulation
- Adaptive behaviour, social skills or social communication.[49]

Ideally, a multidisciplinary team assesses the child, and then a paediatrician makes the diagnosis. Unfortunately, not only in regional and remote areas but throughout Australia, there are insufficient health services to cope with the number of children who need assessment. However, looking at the above list, you can easily imagine how a deficit in three areas would make school and life challenging. A FASD diagnosis alone will not qualify for disability support with Education Queensland, although associated speech-language difficulties may.[50] Additional health professionals and teachers are needed to provide sufficient support. The point of a diagnosis is to provide the appropriate assistance, and unfortunately, as a nation, we fail to do this.

Simon's story (FASD)

Simon is thirteen years old and has low average achievement at school. His teachers know he is clumsy – but they do not realise he has a significant disability. They know he is hyperactive, has poor impulse control and can 'fly off the handle', but staff attribute these to behavioural problems. Their expectations are for a 'normal' thirteen-year-old boy. However, Simon has FASD. He is at a significant disadvantage as his emotional understanding is at eight years, and the idea that 'he acts his age' is unrealistic. This misunderstanding is compounded when he receives age-appropriate consequences for a skill he does not have.

This punitive approach does not assist with building skills but results in anger, the destruction of relationships and potential disengagement from the school system. Continual repetitions of this process can lead to contact with the Justice System, mental health issues and suicide. A study in the United States found that 29.2% of males with FASD reported a serious suicide attempt.[51] This was 19.5 times higher than the national average for males.[51]

Deb Evenson and Jan Lutke (1997) developed the Eight Magic Keys for teaching all students, including those with FASD, which provides good guidelines. The keys are listed below. They identified the 'master key' as trusting relationships.[52]

1. Structure: The glue that makes their world make sense – their foundation
2. Concrete Terms: Talk in concrete terms – avoid abstract language
3. Consistency: Parents and educators use the same words and strategies
4. Repetition: Re-teach many times to retain in long-term memory
5. Routine: Helps reduce anxiety
6. Simplicity: Keep it short and sweet
7. Specific Language: Say exactly what you mean. Give step-by-step directions
8. Supervision: Scaffold independence.[52]

Challenges to change

If schools have inflexible rules such as 'students must not be outside the classroom during lesson time', 'no fidgets in the classroom', and 'everyone sits at their desk', they can be very restrictive and not meet the regulation needs of many students. If emotional regulation and behavioural change are the goals, the courage to review these traditional rules is needed. The cost of maintaining these approaches must be considered. How are other students and the teacher impacted when a meltdown occurs? How many incidents can at least be partly attributed to sensory or regulation needs not being accommodated? Could the outcome have been different with a different approach?

Some may feel that health concerns and diagnoses are not part of what a teacher needs to know and that there are too many different diagnoses to make it practical to learn about them all. However, many diagnoses have overlapping symptoms, and strategies that are useful for one, are often also useful for another. There are also whole-of-class strategies that benefit every student.

It is only possible to meet students' needs by knowing their challenges. Emotional dysregulation is the likely outcome if the child is constantly frustrated or their sensory or emotional needs are not met. From a social justice perspective, the challenges and needs of children and young people who don't have a standard operating system must be understood so they can be provided with equitable access to education.

The table below shows some common and overlapping symptoms and some broad strategies that may be helpful. Remember that many difficulties are symptoms. They are not character flaws or chosen behaviours.

Symptoms	Strategies
Easily distracted	Use seating arrangements to limit distractions
Developmental dysmaturity	Developmentally appropriate expectations and consequences
Difficulty initiating, organising and completing tasks	Reduce anxiety Develop a simple step-by-step process Scaffold independence
Interrupts/intrudes	Calmly remind of rules
Impulsivity	Remind: Stop, Think, Do Games such as 'Simon Says' help
Difficulty with transitions	Consistent routines where possible Give time warning before changes Use fun and humour to relieve anxiety

Symptoms	Strategies
Hyperactive	Movement breaks Heavy work, e.g. take a pile of books to library
Lack of eye contact	Eye contact is not necessary
Lying about the obvious	Humour can be helpful rather than confrontation
Speech & language delays	Appropriate supports
Escalation in response to stress	Aim for a calm and connected classroom Prevention activities
Difficulty seeing cause and effect	Matter-of-fact correction Concise statement of cause and effect
Difficulty with relationships	Increase connection with the child
Manages time poorly	Use of timers and timetables
Often argues with adults	Clear, concise instructions Don't buy into arguments Stay calm
Often blames others for mistakes	Clear, calm statement of responsibility without emotion, and move on
Anxiety	Routine A calm, connected classroom
Sensory issues	Meet sensory needs

Your challenge, should you choose to accept it, is ...

1. If one of your students has a diagnosis, check out the *DSM-V* (2013) criteria.

2. Consider how these issues would make learning, social interactions or emotional regulation challenging.

3. Consider how your school and your classroom mitigate or exacerbate these challenges.

CHAPTER 4

LIVING IN THE STORM

Chloe's story: *Chloe arrives at school late (again). She hangs around the door, not going in. Suddenly a teacher walking past tells her abruptly, 'You're already late. Hurry up and get to class.' Chloe's heart races, and her palms are sweaty. She looks for an escape. The teacher's brusqueness further triggered her autonomic nervous system. She is torn between getting in trouble if she stays out here – and the scariness of being the focus of attention when she walks in. There is no safe place. Chloe stays near the door. Hyperalert. She is watching everything. A teacher's aide sees her there and gently tries to encourage her to come and join the class. She silently refuses.*

The idea that children should be ready and able to learn when they come to school disadvantages many students. Regardless of age, numerous students navigate complex home lives every day. Their responsibilities may include getting themselves awake and organised for school, caring for parents or siblings with physical or mental health challenges, or negotiating life with aggressive and alcohol or drug-affected adults. Many students have the hidden scars of developmental trauma, and their families, whom we may view as 'dysfunctional,' may have struggles we cannot imagine. This situation presents dual difficulties: firstly, the impact of their current environment and secondly, early trauma and toxic stress have potentially harmed their physical, emotional and cognitive development.

Students cannot learn effectively when their fight, flight or freeze systems are activated. Something that happened before going to school may have triggered these protective systems, or a history of trauma may mean they are constantly activated. It is important that all staff understand what this means for the child so that they do not unintentionally add to their experience of trauma and trigger emotional storms. Knowing what trauma is and how it can affect the brain, and how the body reacts can increase compassion and lessen the possibility of taking the students' behaviour personally. This understanding will also reduce frustrations triggered by thoughts that the child is being deliberately difficult. Increased awareness will allow adjustments to teaching practices to meet the student's needs. Knowing the prevalence of trauma – for students, parents and teachers – will reinforce the importance of this knowledge for all people working with children.

The importance of our awareness is highlighted by this quote from O'Hagan (2006):

'Emotional abuse impedes emotional development. In babies, it also impedes the onset of speech development. It retards the process through which a child acquires the ability to feel and express different emotions appropriately and, eventually, to regulate and control them. It impacts adversely on (a) the child's educational, social, and cultural development; (b) psychological development; (c) relationships in adulthood; and (d) career prospects.' [53] [(46)]

A systematic review of literature in Australia revealed that most teachers, both newly graduated and experienced, lacked the confidence and knowledge needed to teach and support students experiencing trauma.[54] Their workload and lack of time to pursue the relevant information compounded the issue.[54] A lack of knowledge can bring feelings of helplessness and hopelessness about a child's situation and behaviour, leading to vicarious trauma, burnout, and leaving the profession.

Supportive relationships are a protective factor in the face of trauma, and often students find these at school. Without understanding trauma, you may misread a child pushing you away as they do not like you or do not want your support. However, it may reflect their struggles with achieving a healthy attachment relationship in early life. One caring adult can make a difference, but those that most need a positive relationship can be the ones that are most challenging and test our resolve. Without a relationship, teaching can be difficult. Your efforts to gain control may cause the child to 'lose it'.

Trauma

Trauma is the emotional, psychological and physiological residue left from heightened stress accompanying experiences of threat, violence and life-challenging events.[55] Traumatic experiences overwhelm our coping capacity.[55] A range of personal and environmental variables influence our ability to cope, so what is traumatic to one person, may not be to another. The support network available during or shortly after the event is an important factor.

There are many types of traumas. These include:

- Single event trauma
- Complex trauma and developmental trauma
- Historical, collective and intergenerational trauma
- Vicarious or secondary trauma
- 'Little t trauma' which includes traumatic events such as the death of a loved one, job loss, the end of a relationship, etc.

The Adverse Childhood Experiences study

The Adverse Childhood Experiences (ACE) study was conducted in the USA from 1995 to 1997 by the Centers for Disease Control and Prevention (CDC) and Kaiser Permanente. This study has contributed much to our knowledge of the extent of childhood trauma and its long-term impact on health and wellbeing. Everyone, especially those working with children, should be aware of the findings of this study and the follow-up research. Shockingly, over twenty-five years have passed since the CDC released the initial study results, and the knowledge gained still does not inform many of our actions around preventing chronic disease and adverse mental health outcomes, or our understanding of childhood learning difficulties, youth offending behaviour or suicides.

The ACE study had over 17,000 participants, predominantly white and college-educated.[3] Only 36% of participants did not have an adverse childhood experience.[3] In this study, the authors defined adverse childhood experiences (ACEs) as:

- Physical, emotional or sexual abuse
- Emotional or physical neglect

- Alcohol or drug abuse in the household
- An incarcerated household member
- Someone in the home who is chronically depressed, mentally ill or suicidal
- Their mother treated violently
- The parents are separated or divorced.

The study reported on adverse experiences before the participant was 18 and only counted each type of adverse childhood experience once, no matter how many times it occurred. The results showed that the more adverse childhood experiences a person had, the more likely they were to develop social, emotional, cognitive and physical issues.[3]

'Early exposure to child abuse or neglect, family turmoil, neighbourhood violence, extreme poverty, racial discrimination, or other hardships can prime biological systems to become hyper-responsive to adversity. Stress-inducing experiences such as these early in life, particularly for children who are genetically more vulnerable to adverse environments, are associated with an increased risk of lifelong physical and mental health problems, including major depression, addictions, heart disease and diabetes.'
56 (6)

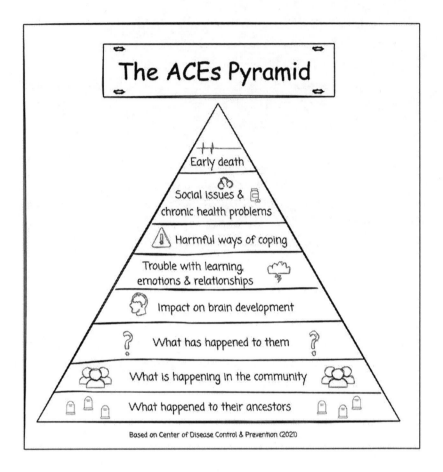

The ACEs Pyramid

- Early death
- Social issues & chronic health problems
- Harmful ways of coping
- Trouble with learning, emotions & relationships
- Impact on brain development
- What has happened to them
- What is happening in the community
- What happened to their ancestors

Based on Center of Disease Control & Prevention (2021)

The ACEs Pyramid

The ACEs Pyramid is a visual representation of the ACE Study. It shows how the experience of ACEs is strongly related to the development of risk factors for a range of health and wellbeing issues throughout life.[3] At the pyramid's base is historical trauma followed by social conditions and local context. These set the foundation and increase the risk for adverse childhood experiences. Adverse childhood experiences then increase the risk of disrupted neurodevelopment, potentially leading to social, emotional and cognitive impairment. These impairments increase the risk of a person adopting health-risk behaviours such as alcohol and drug use, early or unhealthy sexual activity, unhealthy diet, lack of exercise, lack of sleep, and risk-taking behaviours. Health-risk behaviours may lead to increased risk of disease, disability and social problems, and early death resulting from physical or mental health issues.

According to the data, most students, staff and parents have experienced at least one ACE. The impacts most relevant to school years are impaired cognition, behavioural issues and emotional issues that may result from disrupted brain development. Attendance issues may also emerge along with offending behaviour and using alcohol and other drugs as a coping mechanism. Other coping mechanisms may include self-harm and volatile substance misuse.

Schools cannot directly prevent ACEs, but schools are important community institutions contributing to the social conditions and local context. Teachers and staff can be stable and safe people in children's lives.

The impact on your class

The table below shows the percentages that the ACE Study recorded, with the last column indicating what that would look like in a class of 20 students. Due to resilience, available support networks and personality type, not all people who experienced ACEs will be affected similarly. However, the research shows an increased likelihood of adverse outcomes, with the risk increasing as the number of ACEs increase. Another consideration is that this study's participants were predominantly white and college-educated, so presumably, they had a reasonable living standard. Intergenerational trauma and lower socio-economic status are likely to increase these ratios. Research indicates that the rates would be much higher in remote Indigenous communities.

Data from 1st and 2nd Wave of the CDC/Kaiser ACEs Study

Number of ACEs	Percentage of Population	In a Class of 20 (approx.)
0	36.1%	7 students
1	26.0%	5 students
2	15.9%	3 students
3	9.5%	2 students
4 or more	12.5%	3 students
	Center for Disease Control & Prevention.[57]	

People often think the study is irrelevant in Australia because it is from the United States. The studies that have been conducted in Australia show alarming statistics. We cannot just ignore that these children are in our classrooms. Kay Ayre and Govind Krishnamoorthy, authors of *Trauma-Informed Behaviour Support: A Practical Guide to Developing Resilient Learners*, collated data from various studies in their book, some of which is shown in the following table.

Percentage of Australian children subject to different types of maltreatment:	In a Class of 20 (approx.)
Emotional maltreatment 9 to 14%	Between 1 and 3 students
Neglect 1.6 to 4%	Maybe 1 student
Physical abuse 5 to 18%	Between 1 and 4 students
Exposure to family violence 4 to 23%	Between 1 and 5 students
Sexually abused penetrative (male) 1.4 to 7.5%	Maybe 1 or 2 students
Sexually abused non-penetrative (male) 5.2 to 12%	Between 1 and 3 students

Percentage of Australian children subject to different types of maltreatment:	In a Class of 20 (approx.)
Sexually abused penetrative (female) 4 to 12%	Between 1 and 3 students
Sexually abused non-penetrative (female) 10.5 to 21.8 % [58] [(39-40)]	Between 2 and 4 students

These statistics are staggering and sad, and the rules of probability indicate that some of these children will be in your class. Reflecting on what abuse and neglect mean to young students will give an understanding of the origins of some of their behaviour. For some students, it will not be a historical event but something they are currently experiencing. Imagine going to school and pretending everything is okay after being sexually abused. Everyone thinks you only have concerns that are a normal part of childhood. They wonder why you get angry or upset quickly or hide under the desk for no apparent reason. It is unlikely that the child will say anything. Bessel Van der Kolk advises:

'Traumatised children rarely discuss their fears and traumas spontaneously. They also have little insight into the relationship between what they do, what they feel and what has happened to them.' [59] [(405)]

Children are naturally protective of their families, and it takes a great deal of trust before a disclosure is made. It is essential to be aware of your school's reporting procedures. The first step is to listen and ensure safety. Being believed makes an enormous difference in recovery. It is important not to make promises you cannot keep, such as agreeing not to tell anyone.

When working with children, we must be aware of the 'red flags' that may alert us that something is not right, while remembering that they are signals to take notice of and are not diagnostic of abuse. Many of the 'red flags' also occur for other reasons.

Red Flags: Child at Risk of Harm[60]			
Physical Abuse	**Emotional Abuse**	**Sexual Abuse**	**Neglect**
Bruises, welts, burns	Lack of trust in people	Frequent toilet visits	Low weight for age
Family & domestic violence in household	Aggressive, bullying	Sexual knowledge and behaviour not age-appropriate	Stealing food
	Extreme attention-seeking behaviour		Poor hygiene
Unexplained injuries	Overly eager to please adults	Disclosure – directly or indirectly	Sores or health needs unattended
Physically assaults others	Suicide threats or attempts	Unexplained money or gifts	Indiscriminately seeks adult affection
Not attending school because of injury	Persistent running away from home	Concern about an adult the child spends time with	Poor school attendance or often not collected to go home
Injury not consistent with explanation	Highly self-critical, anxious or depressed	Changes in behaviour and/or regressive behaviour	Inadequately supervised for age and culture
Parents' use of excessive discipline	Feelings of worthlessness	Suicide threats or attempts	Rocking; sucking or headbanging

Many schools are moving towards a Trauma-Informed Model of Education. However, this is often more in theory and policy than reality due to the issues mentioned earlier, i.e. a lack of training, knowledge and confidence, time, sufficient staff, etc. Successfully implementing this model will take a holistic and systems-wide approach with adequate support and funding. We all need to advocate for this.

Developmental trauma

Developmental trauma is when the developing brain has been traumatised by neglect, abuse, separation or exposure to violence in the home. It is not yet a *DSM-V* diagnosis but currently fits under complex post-traumatic stress disorder. When exposed to trauma, the developing brain is overwhelmed, and it prioritises the need to survive. Developmental trauma is intimately linked to adverse childhood experiences; however, not everyone exposed to ACEs will have developmental trauma.

As discussed in Chapter 2, each section of the brain has periods that are critical to its development. The timing of the trauma will determine the area of the brain impacted the most; however, remember that the timings are a simplified model and that much development will take place on either side of the timings given. The cortical brain will not be fully developed until about the age of twenty-five years. Although rewiring can happen throughout life, allowing healing and integration, the earlier the disruption of development occurs, the harder it is to heal.

Depending on when the trauma occurred, there will be different impacts. If the disruption occurs during brainstem development, there might be difficulty with concentration and attention. If it occurs when the sensory-motor and survival areas are developing, the child may be overwhelmed by a noisy and busy classroom, have difficulty throwing and catching a ball, have poor handwriting and pencil grip, and have trouble with coordination and balance. They may shut down and zone out frequently throughout the day. There also may be other reasons for these issues and behaviours, and we need to view any behaviour with curiosity rather than jump to conclusions.

Teachers are not immune to struggles that have resulted from adverse childhood experiences. Just like everyone else, they may have trauma histories. Navigating the waters around adverse childhood experiences and developmental trauma can be tricky as a child's story can trigger unprocessed memories for adults at the school. It is also a sensitive issue for parents because they fear blame and judgement. Empathy and compassion can mean that parents are more open to allowing you to know the potential causes of a child's struggles and are more willing to work with you to support the child.

Intergenerational trauma

Intergenerational trauma occurs when the trauma experienced by a previous generation is transmitted to successive generations. This process has biological and environmental components.[61]

While intergenerational trauma is a significant issue for Indigenous people, it can impact non-Indigenous families also. No race or group of people are immune. Australia is built on a history of trauma. Some examples include the shipping of convicts to a faraway country in abysmal conditions, forced adoption of babies of single mothers and forcibly sending children to Australia after World War II.[62] Intergenerational trauma may also occur on a personal level.

Intergenerational trauma for Indigenous families

Shannan Dodson, a Yawuru woman, has this to say about intergenerational trauma:

The high rates of poor physical health, mental health problems, addiction, incarceration, domestic violence, self-harm and suicide in Indigenous communities are directly linked to experiences of trauma. These issues are both results of historical trauma and causes of new instances of trauma, which together can lead to a vicious cycle in Indigenous communities.[63]

To effectively support the Indigenous children in your class, it is helpful to understand why many Indigenous families still suffer the impact of trauma that happened to the generations before them.

Following colonisation, generations of Aboriginal people have suffered collective trauma resulting from the frontier killing times and associated atrocities.[64] They had their lives managed under the *Aboriginals Protection and Restriction of the Sale of Opium Act (1897)* and bore the loss of their land and way of life. The trauma continued for the next generation, who suffered further dispossession, forced removal of children and assimilation. They were denied human rights, wages were stolen, and every aspect of their lives was controlled. Racism and social, economic and health disadvantages continue to impact the daily lives of many.

The transgenerational effects of this trauma include the impact on attachment relationships with caregivers, which in turn affects parenting and family functioning.[65,66] The situation is exacerbated and perpetuated by high-stress levels and trauma associated with multiple bereavements, family and community violence, and racism.[66]

Below are some short excerpts to show a small part of the historical context from Normanton, where I live and work. These stories are repeated all over the country.

'The period from 1868 until 1875 came to be known as "shooting time" or "no good time" in Kurtijar oral histories. Skull Hole is believed to be the site of a large massacre during this period.

73

Originally seven traditional groups were referred to. However, traditional boundaries were fractured by frontier violence and the establishment of pastoralism in the Gulf. In 1874, the local Police Magistrate considered that kidnapping Aboriginal women and children for labour and "immoral" purposes had become institutionalised in Normanton.' [67]

'By the time the Aboriginal Protection and Restriction of the Sale of Opium Act 1897 (the Act) was introduced, opium addiction was already problematic in the Aboriginal community in Normanton. The payment of Aboriginal labourers in opium ash was common and caused severe health problems, adding to the introduced disease problems. The Act had little effect on the opium supply and mainly facilitated the legalised removal of Aboriginal people from their traditional lands.' [67]

'The government forcibly removed many children from the Gulf of Carpentaria region to Mapoon when the mission became an Industrial School under the Industrial and Reformatory Schools Act (1865) (Qld) in 1901. Mapoon's status as an Industrial School meant it became an official location for institutionalising Aboriginal children forcibly removed from their parents under this legislation.' [68]

Intergenerational resilience, healing and love

Despite the trauma, many Indigenous families have survived and thrived, bringing up strong and proud young people. This favourable outcome is not to say that intergenerational trauma has not impacted them; instead, they have had the strength and resilience to endure. Protective factors include extensive kinship systems, cultural and spiritual strengths, and traditionally strong child-rearing practices. [66]

Your challenge, should you choose to accept it, is ...

1. Be aware of the 'red flags' that may indicate child abuse.

2. Ensure you know your school's policies and procedures for reporting concerns.

3. Research the Aboriginal and colonisation history of the area in which you live.

CHAPTER 5

INFLUENCING THE WEATHER

*S*tella's story: *Oh no! It can't be that time already! I've hardly slept! Just five more minutes …*

'Wake up, Mum! It's nearly school time.' Sh!t! Not even time to ring in sick! You guys get ready; I will make breakfast. Don't muck around. We'll be late. Kids and animals fed – tick. Kids to day-care and school – tick. Me to class – tick. A rush, but we did it! However, once I had a moment to stop, I thought – I should have gone to the bathroom before I arrived. It is a long time until the break. And what about my lunch? I left that *and my water bottle on the bench. Oh well. Not to worry. Not the first time. I will be okay.*

The class comes in. They are noisy and take ages to settle. Many students seem set on pushing my buttons this morning. I can feel myself becoming annoyed and impatient. How long until the break? I should have had my morning coffee.

Most people are unaware of how much they influence the 'weather' around them and how effectively they could manage reactions and relationships if they used some simple strategies. Teachers often have the power to avert emotional storms or limit their impact through verbal and non-verbal communication. However, to do this, the relevant knowledge and skills need to be acquired along with an awareness of what we communicate.

For a teacher, one of the significant benefits of influencing the weather in your classroom is the confidence it gives you to be in charge of your ship: to know that it will not flounder on the rocks because an unexpected storm has materialised. It is also not going to be becalmed by a lack of energy. You can up-regulate your class when they are in the doldrums and down-regulate when needed.

As mentioned previously, adults need to model self-regulation to students and support their regulation, as they require many experiences of co-regulation before they can effectively self-regulate. Even as adults, we need others to help us regulate at times of great stress. Teachers have a significant role in supporting children to gain these skills by maintaining their calm in the face of a storm. This level of regulation is easier said than done. However, it will assist the child in developing an essential life skill that may not have been modelled sufficiently for the child previously. Students are more likely to feel safe in a calm, well-regulated classroom and will, therefore, learn more effectively.

Being able to keep the class regulated is also protective of your wellbeing. It can feel like you are walking on eggshells, just waiting for an eruption if you do not have confidence in your ability to prevent a student from dysregulating (at least most of the time). If you get heightened by their dysregulation, your stress levels increase, and your ability to say and do things that do not worsen the situation is significantly reduced.

Research by Glazzard and Rose (2020) found evidence that teachers teaching when they were struggling with their own mental health and wellbeing had a detrimental effect on students.[69] Students in this study identified that teachers being at work when struggling impacted their learning and that they responded to the teacher's mood with their behaviour.[69] Further, the teachers identified that their mental health impacted their classroom management capacity, student relationships and teaching practice.[69] When teachers are unwell physically or emotionally, or their mood is low, they influence the weather in the classroom, and emotional storms are more likely. A teacher will struggle to use the suggestions in this chapter if they are not well. This again highlights the need for self-care.

John White and John Gardner, in the book *Classroom X-Factor: the Power of Body Language and Non-Verbal Communication in Teaching*, highlighted that teachers could use such things as facial and vocal expressions, gestures and body language, and eye contact and smiling as ways to better connect with their students and create effective learning experiences.[70] The flip side of this idea is that we can also use facial and vocal expressions, gestures and body language to stop connection and portray our discomfort, disinterest or distress.

Dysregulation, whether it is a student having a meltdown or the teacher yelling or raising their voice, reduces the children's sense of safety in the classroom. For some, especially those who have experienced trauma, it will trigger a fight, flight or freeze response, compounding an already volatile situation. Children are excellent at detecting our emotional tone. Even if we choose our words carefully, our tone and body language can betray us, leaving children feeling unsafe at an unconscious level.

There are multiple ways to influence the weather; putting them all together is a powerful strategy. This chapter will include what to do before you set sail. It will highlight the importance of co-regulation and the intentional use of verbal and non-verbal communication. However, don't forget that you need ongoing self-care to ensure healthy baseline emotional regulation before you start.

Before you greet the crew

Before entering the classroom, you must check that you are okay and have met your physical and wellbeing needs. This strategy sounds basic but I know many teachers do not get to eat properly at school, and their restroom needs are often not prioritised. It is worth considering how this can be different as a school or teacher cohort. All these contribute to your ability (or inability) to regulate and assist others in regulating. Ensuring you meet your physical and wellbeing needs improves your ability to ride the little waves. You are then prepared for any storms that may develop during the session.

Do a body scan: Start from your head and move down your body. Notice areas of tension. Breathe into them and let them relax. Our shoulders, jaws and foreheads often hold our tension, so pay particular attention to these. The more often you do a body scan, the more conscious you will become of the building tension in your body. Body awareness is essential for regulation, for both teachers and students. People have often spent years blocking the messages from their bodies. Now is the time to start noticing and improving your 'set point of wellbeing'.[71] If you are already tense, it will not take much to push you outside your window of tolerance.[19]

Be aware of your posture, facial expressions and voice: Most of what we communicate is not in words – it is in our body language and the tone of our voice, its volume and inflection. Our non-verbal communication can transmit a sense of safety and connection or unpredictability and danger to students. Softening your facial expression and ensuring that your tone invites connection and participation, rather than activating a fight-or-flight response, will make for a more productive and pleasant day for you and your students. What we say must align with what students are reading from our body language because if they don't match, this can create a sense of unpredictability.

Our posture says so much, not only to the students, but to *our* brains and nervous systems as well. When stressed or overwhelmed, our body sags, and our shoulders, neck and head reflect our feelings. While we must be authentic, and we need to experience our emotions, we don't want to be stuck in them or overwhelmed by them. We can change how we feel by taking a breath, changing our posture and softening our gaze. Sometimes we need to come across as strong despite how we feel inside, for our safety or to support someone else. Using our posture and knowledge of body language, we can communicate and tap into our strengths. I teach bullied students to 'walk away strong' with their heads up and shoulders back. We role-play and practise this, noticing how it changes how the bully feels and how we feel inside. While this is nowhere near the answer to bullying, or a magic potion when we feel overwhelmed, it is a simple but powerful strategy.

How we look at or focus on people can make them feel safe or uncomfortable. An intense gaze can trigger a fight or flight response, while soft eyes support connection and cooperation. Soft eyes combine our focused and detailed vision with our peripheral vision, and it takes practice to achieve. Using *'soft eyes and a warm heart'* [72] changes our perception and how others perceive us.

Our voice also communicates so much more than *what* we say. Dependent on the listener's trauma history, experiences, auditory processing ability and hearing, what we intend to communicate can get lost or translated into something completely different.

With the *volume* of our voice, we can make someone feel safe and connected or trigger the fight, flight or freeze response. Our volume can transfer our emotions to others, hurt the ears of someone with auditory sensitivities, demand attention or exclude someone with hearing loss from the conversation. With the *tone* of our voice, we can command attention, build connections (or break them), induce calm or panic, encourage collaboration, and so much more. Vocal tone is one of the most potent ways to support a neuroception of safety.[73] With the *rate* of our speech, we can indicate urgency, make people feel calm or rushed and overwhelmed, and increase or decrease understanding for people with hearing loss or auditory processing difficulties.

After using strategies to calm the class, you can burst this bubble of calm by the tone and volume of speech used to direct children back to their desks. While using a 'teacher's voice' can assert authority, it does not keep children in a calm space if this is the aim. We can easily trigger the nervous system's alarm response by not considering the impact of our voice on the class. On the other hand, a calm and soothing voice would not be appropriate if you were trying to raise the level of energy in the classroom, as you would require a more fun and upbeat approach. Our voice is a powerful tool to use to help maintain regulation.

Mikki is a child with FASD who also has moderate hearing loss. Her behaviours, hyperactivity and impulsivity, test the patience of even the most tolerant of teachers. Mikki does try — but her ability to maintain this is severely limited. Most lessons end with the teacher sending her out of the classroom. Mikki is pretty okay with this, as by that time, both she and the teacher need a break. What she struggles with is when someone yells at her. Mikki tells a trusted person that it hurts her ears. She did try telling the teacher, but that resulted in further yelling as the teacher thought she was being cheeky. She tried covering her ears to prevent the pain. Again, this antagonised the situation rather than improving it.

So how does a child get an adult to listen? What they say may come across as cheeky, but it may also be true. It is easy to rebuke the child for their disability inadvertently.

A mindfulness strategy: As you walk into your classroom, be mindful of the new space you are entering. Take a breath and notice your new environment and what it holds. It is common to be so immersed in your thoughts that you don't see these things. Are you able to pay attention to the 'here and now' instead of thinking about what happened in the last lesson or what you need to do for the next class? Moving flexibly from the activities of the mind to engaging purposefully with at least one of your five senses reduces the likelihood of becoming 'stuck' in your thoughts and feelings. Notice what you see as you enter – with soft eyes. Notice the connections and relationships you have in the room and nurture these.

If you use these strategies yourself, you will be more confident and competent at sharing them with a student when they are needed.

Synchronising systems: Co-regulation and mirror neurons

> 'Children learn how to regulate their emotions through "co-regulation". The better we can soothe them when they are agitated or support them when they are low, the better they "absorb" how to do this for themselves.'[32]

We are social beings, and we continually pick up on and potentially reflect the feelings of others, using what is theorised to be mirror neurons. I am sure you have noticed a sense of negativity within a particular group while experiencing positive and enthusiastic vibes within other groups. As mentioned previously, mums often find that when they are not feeling well or are stressed, this will be when their children press every button they have. A mum's wellbeing influences the children's emotional state – and vice versa. We notice that we feel more relaxed in the company of calm people. We also have a bodily reaction when people are angry or agitated. Our flight system gets activated. You will notice that when people are arguing, and somebody starts to talk louder, the other person is likely to also speak louder. Anger transmits from one person to another very quickly. Their emotions heighten, their voice gets louder, their breathing gets quicker and shallower, and their heart beats faster. Our survival has depended on our social connections and being able to read one another. We are mostly very good at it, but sometimes this is not an advantage. A minor incident can escalate quickly unless at least one party can self-regulate.

It's essential to notice how the child is 'making' you feel in these instances. This feeling can give you a hint as to how they are feeling. We are aiming to use our mirror neurons to help regulate the child. They also use their mirror neurons to communicate, so if you notice that you are feeling helpless in a particular situation or you're feeling frightened, not good enough or doubting your ability as a teacher to control the situation, they may be having similar feelings and this may be what they are communicating. Maybe they are feeling helpless or frightened or unable to be good enough. Children often intensify their efforts to express their feelings if you don't understand them. They will regulate much more quickly if they know you get it, and 'name it to tame it'.[74] If you notice you are being sucked into their storm, take a breath. Model self-regulation strategies. If you cannot regulate, take a break and say, 'We can talk about this later' – not threateningly – but in a supportive way. Offer the child a break to go for a walk and get a drink. You both need time and space to get out of your 'emotional brains' and back into your thinking and problem-solving brains.

Sometimes people are unwilling to adapt their behaviour or approach to cater to the other person's needs and expect the other person to adapt to their way – an 'accept me as I am approach'. However, this often does not end well, especially when the other person is a child with a developing regulation system. Not being aware of how verbal and non-verbal communication impacts students can exacerbate the situation and contribute to emotional storms in the classroom. The tone and volume of the teachers' voice can mean that some of the most vulnerable students are constantly in fight, flight or freeze mode, and a minor happening can push them overboard.

Anger and chaos can be contagious in the classroom, but so are happiness, fun, motivation, smiles, and an atmosphere of learning. You are the ship's captain and must be prepared when you step on board. Prioritise your needs. There will be occasions when things go awry, like for Stella at the start of this chapter, but this would be the exception rather than a way of life. All teachers have been there and know that expecting things to go well when unprepared is like wishing on a rainbow. However, it is still possible to achieve a day of learning with an awareness of your body language and other non-verbal communication, some strategies to avert storms, and an ability to up and down-regulate the energy in the classroom. In the scenario surrounding Stella, the energy is high, and children are taking ages to settle. Stella could consider two approaches. She could start with a high-energy and fun music and movement activity to eliminate their wriggles and then end with a slower (60 beats per minute) song to bring their heart rate down and calm them. Alternatively, Stella may use a mindfulness activity or tapping to settle the class and prepare them to learn. Either approach would also benefit Stella if she actively took part. It would synchronise their systems and aid positive, supportive relationships.

> *'The muscles used to make a smile send a biochemical message to our nervous system that it is safe to relax the flight or freeze response.'* [75]

Your challenge, should you choose to accept it, is ...

- Take notice of your body language when you enter the classroom.
- Take note of what feelings arise when a child dysregulates.
- Have a plan for those days when things start badly.
    - What music or activity would you use to gain a better start to the day?

CHAPTER 6

CONNECT WITH
THE CREW

Amy's Story: *I don't know what else I can do. I have tried to form a relationship with Codi, but when I think I have a connection with her, she totally rejects me: pushing me away, swearing at me and saying hurtful things. It is tough to connect with someone who treats you like that. I notice she is pretty isolated from her peers, also. When she does connect with someone, she becomes clingy and possessive, which ultimately pushes them away. At times she appears manipulative and coercive in her relationships, both with her peers and the adults who try to connect with her. In class, she continually demands the attention of adults; if she does not get it, she will act as the class clown or escalate confrontation to maintain the attention of others. I don't understand why she still behaves this way when I have put so much effort into establishing a connection with her.*

Establishing connections with some students can be hard work with few short-term rewards. However, to captain the boat successfully, you need to get to know and connect with your crew, acknowledging that for some, this may take much persistence over an extended period. Strong and positive connections to the school and staff are essential for all children and an important protective factor for vulnerable children. A child's relationship with their teacher will influence their behaviour, the respect they show and their ability to regulate within the classroom. With a positive and supportive relationship, a teacher is much more likely to be able to give corrective feedback without precipitating a storm.

Students are curious and open to learning when in a 'safe and social' state. In the last chapter, we looked at increasing students' sense of safety through verbal and non-verbal communication. This chapter will show how this foundation of safety lays the groundwork for establishing strong relationships that support learning and wellbeing. The strength of these relationships can change lives through the education it facilitates and by providing a template for students' future relationships. Relationships at school can give a second chance at establishing a secure attachment style. However, relationships cannot be behaviour dependant. They must be based on unconditional positive regard (UPR).[76]

Dr Dan Siegel tells us that the primary carers' relationship with their child is so vital that it shapes the structure and function of their child's brain.[19] We know that brain development does not stop when they go to school, and experiences at school also shape the brain. An awareness of the impact of teachers and teaching is crucial.

> *'Our goal with kids is to maintain a connection with their hearts while teaching skills, boundaries and behaviour. If we lose their heart during the process, nothing else will matter.'*[77]

There are many potential issues within a classroom if a teacher does not get to know and connect with their crew. When students do not have a connection with their teacher, they are likely to lack trust, and their sense of safety will be compromised. This insecurity will impact their ability to try new things and accept mistakes as part of learning. When a child does not feel seen and understood by the teacher, they are likely to ramp up their behaviours until they are recognised. If you do not know and understand a student's strengths inside and outside the classroom, you cannot teach the whole child and capitalise on these attributes. Without some knowledge of the student's circumstances, you can inadvertently trigger resentment and anger. Examples of when this may occur include when a child whose mother has passed away is not supported when the class is doing Mother's Day activities or when a student whose Dad physically abuses them is contacted for a misdemeanour at school. We cannot avoid some of these issues due to information not being shared. However, a trusting relationship will make it more likely for the student or parent to share concerns.

'Strong student-teacher relationships inspire student collaboration in maintaining a safe and positive learning environment. Often, what is characterised as misbehaviour is really a conflict between a student and a teacher. Creating a classroom where students feel safe and seen, where there is greater comfort and less conflict, can prevent or reduce behaviour problems.' [78 (50)]

Strong relationships and attachment

Strong relationships are the key to learning and behavioural management. If you can achieve this, it will minimise many other issues. However, for children to connect, they first need to feel safe. Children's trauma and attachment histories will impact how well they can form relationships. Often the children who need to connect the most will be the ones who continually push us away, let us into their world and then reject us, or who become over-clingy and dependent.

There are many reasons why a child may not develop secure attachment, e.g. Mum suffering from post-natal depression, either parent having a mental illness including addiction, death of a parent, separation from their carer due to illness, trauma, lack of parenting skills, etc. The following section is a brief overview of attachment styles. There are more complex ways to view attachment styles, and we know that children (and adults) may default to a different style depending on the relationship, so people can't just be put in a box. When reflecting on your relationship with a particular student, it is helpful to remember that we all have an attachment style and it impacts our ability to form a relationship with others.

A child is likely to have developed a *secure attachment style* if, in their early development, a carer met their physical and emotional needs promptly and consistently. These children can be soothed if distressed, have confidence and feel worthy of love. They can be attentive, problem-solve, take risks, and seek and receive help.[79] They have a positive and open way of interacting with others and actively engage in learning.

A child might have developed an *insecure ambivalent attachment style* if the caregiver was inconsistent and unpredictable in the care and comfort they provided. As a result, the child may be oversensitive to feelings of rejection and experience separation anxiety. This child may constantly seek the teacher's attention. If they do not get it, they may muck around to get the attention (connection) needed or escalate confrontation to maintain attention.[79] Their relationships may oscillate between connection-seeking and pushing away and between characterising the person as all good or all bad.[79] They may appear coercive or manipulative in their relationships. They may be clingy and possessive with their peers, making it hard for them to maintain friendships. As a result, they are sometimes very isolated.

You may recognise Amy's student Codi in this description. If you can identify a child's attachment style or styles, it may present you with strategies that help establish a relationship. It also offers ways to increase the child's sense of safety so that they can learn more effectively.

Codi needs kindness and nurturing while being supported to manage for short periods without constant attention.[79] Amy can help Codi by ensuring she has consistent, but not constant, adult support. Amy or a teacher aide could provide this by noticing Codi frequently and gradually increasing her time working independently. Using a timer will reduce her anxiety by making the time of working independently predictable. There is safety in predictability. Breaking tasks into smaller chunks and planning regulation activities rather than waiting for dysregulation can be very helpful. Providing predictable routines and visual timetables can increase safety and learning for children like Codi.

A child might have developed an *insecure avoidant attachment* style if the caregiver was distant and rejecting of the child and their needs. This child may appear happy or settled most of the time, and they may deny their distress or fail to communicate it. They are often withdrawn and quiet but may appear more independent and self-reliant than you would expect for their age. They may be reluctant to seek help from adults. These children may have a fear of failure and appear emotionally distant. If they become stressed, they have a sudden and inexplicable explosion and then recover quickly.[79]

A teacher can help by planning clear, concrete, structured tasks and ensuring that games have clear rules.[79] It is helpful to start with games that do not have winners or losers – games that are purely for fun. To encourage a child to accept help, look for opportunities to nurture and avoid encouraging this child to cope with things independently. For most children, encouraging independence is the goal but this child needs to learn that it is safe to accept help. Characters in stories can be used to help explore emotions. This child may have low arousal. Activities that involve swinging, rolling and spinning can help if this is an issue. Self-esteem is often lacking, so anything that can improve self-concept is important. These children may struggle with getting things wrong and need support to know it is okay not to be perfect.[79]

A child might have developed a *disorganised attachment style* if the caregiver was frightened of or frightening to the child. While the child may be anxious, distressed, afraid and insecure, their behaviours may vary from being aggressive to being withdrawn and over-compliant.[79] Their anxiety may present as controlling behaviour, and they may bully, provoke and challenge others to stay in control.[79] Their need to be in control may mean they have few friends. They are often hyper-aroused and disruptive in class. Their poor stress tolerance can impact relationships and learning and compound their tendency to resist help from teachers and others. These behaviours developed as adaptive responses to keep them safe or meet their needs. The problem is that they no longer serve them well – at least not in the school environment.

A strategy that is helpful to all children is helping the child feel safe within the classroom by providing a calm, predictable environment. For children displaying a disorganised attachment style, having a quiet, safe place with regulation activities available to them when needed can be helpful. Ideally, an adult with whom they have a positive relationship would be available. Addressing the whole class to give instructions rather than directly speaking to them can reduce stress. Maintaining an empathetic, calm and non-confrontational approach will achieve the best results when correcting the child. When the child needs to regulate, puzzles and sensory activities can be helpful. Rhythmical physical movement can reduce stress and help the child to regulate.

'Safe and social'

> *'Emotional regulation flows naturally from being in the presence of someone we trust.'* [80]

All children should feel safe in the classroom, but often they don't, and it is not necessarily about you. This feeling relates to a *neuroception* of safety, a 'felt sense' rather than actual safety. There may be things in the environment that trigger fear for the child; it may be a raised voice or a loud noise, or how someone moves towards them that triggers their alert system. It could also be something as vague as a smell. The child may not be aware of what the trigger is – or why it is a trigger – as it may be hidden deep in their memory.

The relationship between students and teachers is integral, as a child learns most effectively in a 'safe and social' state.[4] As mentioned previously, some children have not had the opportunity to experience safe and connected relationships, and the school community provides a second opportunity for children to establish a secure attachment.[81] Research shows that when faced with adverse childhood experiences, the children who do well have at least one adult who provides a safe, supportive and stable relationship.[82] Often, this safe and supportive adult is a school staff member.

Historical events, as well as what has happened recently, impact a child's neuroception of safety. It relies on an instantaneous subconscious processing of safety and risks. Neuroception will determine a child's state – safe and social, fight or flight, or freeze. To increase a neuroception of safety, teachers can provide a calm and predictable environment. They can make the unknown known by telling the students what the plan is for the session and having visual timetables and reminders. Ensuring the child knows what they should do if upset or angry, where they can go, and whom they should see is essential.

There are often plans for students with a diagnosis, such as those with ADHD or ASD. However, many others struggle with emotional regulation and don't have a diagnosis. They may have problems with emotional regulation related to delayed development or lack of exposure to environments that allow them to develop the capacity to regulate, or it may relate to the experience of trauma.

93

According to Polyvagal Theory, the autonomic nervous system has three primary states.

- Ventral vagal system: Safe and social
- Sympathetic nervous system: Fight or flight
- Dorsal vagal system: Freeze or shut down.[4]

This chapter will look at the ventral vagal system, as this is the ideal state for students to be in most of the time for learning. They can move a little down the autonomic nervous system (ANS) ladder to gain some sympathetic nervous system energy, as that can provide the motivation needed to meet a challenge. Still, they need one foot firmly in the ventral vagal state to feel safe enough to try. In this state, they are centred, connected to those around them and curious about what the teacher shares. They have open body language and a relaxed posture. Just as your body language silently communicates with students, noticing their body language can give you hints of what is happening for them. In the ventral vagal state, their hearing tunes in to human voices. They can do creative thinking, problem-solving and collaborate with others – all things essential for learning, particularly in a group environment like a classroom. Students can also effectively engage in art, music, mindfulness and conversations in this state.[73]

As you can see, aiming to help students stay in this state for much of the time is helpful for their learning. However, even the calmest person does not remain in one state all day. Imagine the autonomic nervous system states as a ladder that we go at least partially up and down multiple times daily. We all have our default position on the ladder. If we tend to be anxious – our default position may be between fight and flight and safe and social. We (and our students) also have a default position that we go to when stressed. This position will be 'fight or flight' for some and 'freeze' for others. We will look at these more in Chapter 8.

Unconditional positive regard

Unconditional positive regard (UPR) is a term coined by Carl Rogers, meaning that we accept people as inherently human and lovable without regard to their words or actions.[76] This ideal does not mean we accept everything they do or say, but that these do not take away from their inherent value.

UPR is an essential concept in education, as some students' behaviours can make it difficult to accept them unconditionally. However, understanding where these behaviours have come from and what they may be communicating can aid our acceptance. It is also helpful to recognise that accepting children with unconditional positive regard improves relationships and models behaviour that can create a culture of acceptance within your classroom. If a teacher views a child with unconditional positive regard, it can enhance their image of themselves. This improved image can increase their ability to form positive relationships and improve their behaviour. It is important for adults not to take the words and actions of students too personally. Again, that does not mean the child escaping responsibility, but rather that the matter be dealt with calmly, with curiosity about the causes and with compassion.

Unconditional positive regard can be as simple as greeting each child when they arrive and asking them how they are going, or when a child comes to class late, genuinely welcoming them and refraining from greetings such as 'glad you finally made it' or 'so good of you to get here'.

'Being recognised and affirmed by a powerful adult can be life-changing for a young person.'[83]

Strengths approach

An excellent way to connect with students is by identifying and acknowledging their strengths in the classroom and the real world. These strengths may include skills in sports, art, music, maths, motorbike riding, fishing, playing video games, or character strengths such as being a good friend or being persistent or trustworthy. Their strengths may also include connections to family, culture and country, religious or spiritual group membership, or independence. There are many benefits to building on strengths. You may discover a shared interest or develop a new respect for the student's talent or attributes by talking about these. Your genuine interest in the student as a person will improve your relationship within the classroom and, consequently, the student's sense of safety and emotional regulation. There is evidence that reinforcing and developing a person's strengths achieves better outcomes than 'fixing' deficits.[46]

Establishing relationships

'How do teachers demonstrate responsiveness and build relationships in the classroom? Researcher and author John Gottman suggests that it starts with bids for connection. Bids are attempts to get attention, affirmation, affection or any other positive connection. They can be subtle (like a gesture or facial expression) or overt (like a question or request for help). There are three ways to respond to bids: turning toward, turning against or turning away. To turn toward means to respond in a positive, affirming way, while turning against may look like belittling, being argumentative or being aggressive. Turning against obviously damages relationships, but so does turning away, which involves ignoring a bid. Turning away may be done intentionally, but more often, it happens because we are preoccupied.'[78] (45)

An awareness of your 'turning against' or 'turning away' responses, inadvertent or otherwise, is vital to understanding whether the relationship may need repair. There is no possible way a teacher could notice and attend to every bid for connection in their classroom. Still, as was mentioned earlier, perfection is not what a student needs. Students need a 'good enough' response rate and relationship repair modelled to them. It may be 'sorry I could not get to you sooner', just like we would say if we were serving someone and they had to wait. When waiting for service, we know the person is doing their best, and they cannot help everyone at once. However, it certainly makes a difference to how we respond to waiting if this is acknowledged. As adults, we often do not extend this courtesy to children, which can lead to escalating emotions.

Dan Hughes' PACE Model supports building relationships, particularly for children who have experienced trauma, but is beneficial for everyone. PACE is an attitude or stance of **P**layfulness, **A**cceptance, **C**uriosity and **E**mpathy.[84] These qualities help create emotional safety, and both parties to the conversation stay open and engaged with the other.

> *'Playfulness can diffuse minor behaviours in the classroom; acceptance can reduce defensiveness and opposition within the child/young person; curiosity can allow a student to feel heard and understood; and empathy can help relieve feelings of shame.'* [85]

In years gone by, an authoritarian approach was thought to be the most effective way to gain and maintain control and, therefore, teach. However, while boundaries and routine are essential and necessary, most now recognise that this approach in schools, workplaces or homes is damaging and does not produce the best learning or behaviour and may leave children vulnerable to abuse. Without a safe connection to their teacher, there is an ongoing struggle for the child to feel seen and understood, which can translate into 'attention-seeking' behaviours. It is more helpful to label these behaviours as connection-seeking. We can then see the real need behind them. We tend to pay attention to negative behaviours, especially for a child who displays these often. We are waiting for them to occur. If they happen to be 'good', we don't say anything for fear that we will burst the bubble. Connection is not behaviour dependent. It is wanting to know about their interests, strengths, what they love and hate, what makes them feel safe, and what triggers fear. According to experts in the field, Gabor Maté and Gordon Neufeld, challenging behaviours are a relationship problem rather than a behavioural problem.[86] This highlights the importance of building these relationships if we wish to change behaviours.

An argument against forming strong relationships came up in the research for my thesis. Some teachers identified that they 'did not want to be their friend', and this closely aligned with a concern about boundaries. The idea is not to be 'friends' with a student any more than being a friend is an appropriate role for a parent. The idea is to establish a respectful student-teacher relationship based on genuine care, knowledge, empathy and compassion. This relationship has appropriate boundaries of behaviour for both the student and the teacher. Boundaries create actual safety and a felt sense of safety. In enforcing limits, teachers must remain approachable and human, and be flexible when required.

If you nurture your connection to the students in your class, and there is the inevitable build-up to a storm, you can provide the student with a life raft and be reasonably confident that they will climb aboard and accept the assistance. Without a relationship, the child will likely reject your intervention and figuratively drown rather than board the life raft.

Your challenge, should you choose to accept it, is ...

1. Identify a student with whom you struggle to form a relationship.
2. See if an attachment style may fit with what you observe and experiment with those strategies.
3. Spend some regular short periods of time getting to know and acknowledging the student's strengths.

CHAPTER 7

PRE-SEA TRAINING

James' story: *James has observed that in his class, there is a small core group of students who have difficulty regulating their emotions, and a disproportionate amount of class time is invested in managing their behaviours and emotions. When it was initially suggested that he incorporate regulation activities into his daily timetable, he thought adding another activity to the already crowded curriculum would add to his stress. He opted not to do it, thinking it was not a core responsibility. Lately, he has been reading some research and reflecting on whether prevention may be a better approach, but he is unsure what to do.*

When the weather is calm is when you need to act. It is far easier to prevent emotional storms than to navigate through the dark and stormy seas once they have developed. You also want to train the crew to act when they notice that the weather is changing. Some students, especially those who have experienced trauma, will need to learn to recognise the build-up stage of the storm and how it feels in their bodies. Many will also need to learn the language to express their feelings.

The time spent in prevention activities will pay you back many times and benefit the children you teach and their future families for life. If children learn emotional literacy, body awareness and self-regulating skills and strategies, there is a potential to reduce rates of domestic and family violence, incarceration, mental health issues, and even potentially some suicides. The causes of suicide are multifactorial; however, for many, two factors are dysregulation and impulsivity. While there are impressive arguments for using strategies to achieve a calm brain for learning, there are even stronger ones for supporting children's mental health and wellbeing, along with their physical health, through the mind-body connection. The bonus is that doing these activities with your class will ultimately benefit your wellbeing with a direct effect on your amygdala and stress hormones and an indirect impact through the reduced stress of teaching a calmer class. There are many ways to achieve this outcome.

> 'As educators, we must teach emotional regulation to our students for them to achieve goal-directed and purposeful behaviour. We must equip our students with the ability to self-identify and manage their emotions so that they can make good choices if we expect a positive classroom environment.' [87]

Emotional regulation is a learned skill with important implications for students' academic and social development. Children who have difficulty regulating their emotions have challenges with learning.[88] Dysregulation not only affects the dysregulated child, it also impacts the learning of others. Emotional regulation is not about ignoring or not feeling our emotions. Both of these can lead to unhealthy outcomes. Emotional regulation allows us to notice, feel and interpret our emotions as they arise and then choose how we respond.

Prevention work is essential to prevent collateral damage. Children becoming highly dysregulated is a frightening experience for the teacher, the other students and the child themselves. While many children are exposed to anger and violence every day, we know it is harmful, and most of us try to protect ourselves and our children from this in the community. It is not okay that children, and their teachers, are exposed to this in the school environment. It must be prevented. However, punishing the dysregulated child does not increase their skills and may result in victim blaming. We need another way.

Our brains are wired for connection, so states of regulation can be transmitted within the class or group. We have all noticed how easily chaos can emerge when one or two children dysregulate. This situation can be particularly evident when a relief teacher takes a class. The unplanned change can be enough to unsettle a couple of children, and then there is a cascading effect that impacts many more. You can use your knowledge of collective regulation to go against this trend by staying with the classroom teacher's routine, especially if the class generally starts with a calming ritual. Like all strategies, it is not a magic wand, but being able to replicate the usual calming strategy will give you a positive start. However, to do this, it needs to be part of the everyday routine.

So, the big question is, 'What strategies?' Firstly, let's look at a quote from Bessel Van der Kolk, one of the gurus in this area, and then one from Brené Brown. The strategies suggested as pre-sea training for your crew will include these concepts.

'If you want to manage your emotions better, your brain gives you two options: You can learn to regulate them from the top down

or the bottom up. Top-down regulation involves strengthening the capacity of the watchtower to monitor your body's sensations. Mindfulness meditation and yoga can help with this. Bottom-up regulation involves recalibrating the autonomic nervous system ... we can access the ANS through breath, movement or touch.' [89]

'Research shows that the process of labelling emotional experience is related to greater emotion regulation and psychosocial wellbeing.' [90]

Emotional literacy is the ability to identify emotions within ourselves and others, which then helps us to communicate our thoughts and feelings and have empathy for the feelings of others. Having the skills and the language to express emotions without becoming overwhelmed does not come easily for some children for various reasons. Increasing emotional literacy and body awareness can improve children's ability to regulate and calm their bodies and brains. Dan Siegal's 'name it to tame it' approach or Cathy Malchiodi's 'express it to address it', which broadens the concept to include non-verbal and creative ways of expressing feelings, are effective strategies. However, a child must first be able to identify their emotions accurately. Many children (and adults) will recognise that they are angry but may need assistance to realise that there may be primary feelings of disappointment, frustration or sadness.

Interoception is the awareness of what is happening inside your body. This awareness includes feeling hungry or thirsty, and hot or cold, but also things like muscle tension, heartbeat and soft touch. Interoception is implicated in self-regulation and self-awareness. When someone says their anger goes from 0 to 100 with no warning, usually it is because they cannot 'feel' their bodily sensations like their jaw clenching or their muscles tensing. This awareness is sometimes blocked because of previous trauma. However, it is also a skill that can be practised and improved.

Pre-sea training adventures

You and your class may like to take some of the pre-sea training adventures in this chapter, or you may have your own favourite regulation activity. There is no need to do all of them. However, you may like to experiment before committing to a particular activity. Then, pick one or two that are comfortable for you and commit to doing it consistently with your class. Some, like EFT (tapping), only take a few minutes, and it is ideal to do them a few times a day, maybe at the start of the day and after breaks. Some can be combined easily with others, like tapping and finishing with a breathing exercise. It is crucial that you and all other staff participate. By joining the activity, you are demonstrating the value of it and modelling the behaviour. It will also help you maintain your regulation.

Neuro education

It can be helpful for students to understand some of the basic workings of the brain, particularly relating to emotional regulation and 'flipping your lid'. Dr Dan Siegal provides a great model using the hand to show students the different areas of the brain and what happens when the amygdala is triggered. This model can aid children's understanding of why and how emotional regulation activities work. There are YouTube videos with Dr Siegal demonstrating his model.

Rhythmic activities

'All life is rhythmic. The rhythms of the natural world are embedded in our biological systems. This begins in the womb when the mother's beating heart creates rhythmic sound, pressure and vibrations that are sensed by the developing fetus and provide constant rhythmic input to the organising brain.' [25]

After birth, our constant exposure to rhythm continues with our heartbeat and breathing. When a baby needs calming, we rock it. If we don't get the rhythm right, usually because we are stressed, the baby will not settle. We've all experienced or witnessed a tired and stressed mum trying to soothe her bub without success, and then someone comes along and takes over, and the baby settles. It is all about our rhythms and what we are communicating to the baby.

Tapping (Emotional Freedom Technique – EFT)
Dr Peta Stapleton is a researcher and lecturer at Bond University (Gold Coast) who has researched the effectiveness of the Emotional Freedom Technique (EFT, also known as tapping) as a stress reduction technique for school children. Day-care centres, kindergartens, schools and universities in Australia and overseas have introduced adaptations of the program to suit specific ages. Research conducted in Northern Territory schools shows that tapping reduces anxiety and increases wellbeing.[91] As anxiety underlies many meltdowns and emotional storms, strategies such as these are essential.

The EFT process involves rhythmical tapping on specific points (acupoints) to calm the amygdala. These points are from ancient Chinese wisdom. Research shows that tapping on these points reduces cortisol levels, while tapping on sham points does not.[92] The amygdala is responsible for the 'fight, flight or freeze' response when someone is stressed, distressed or angry. Tapping also involves noticing feelings in your body, being able to name them and rate their intensity. Practising these skills can increase emotional literacy and body awareness over time. It also uses statements of acceptance and affirmation. EFT is evidence-based, has a growing body of research, and each component has its own evidence base.

From my experience, tapping is an excellent technique for young school children, adolescents and adults. I have found that students engage with it well, especially when using a story and puppet to introduce specific emotions. I use my bear, Boris. Boris has a life of his own, and many children ask his whereabouts if he is not with me.

One day, Boris was angry as he called 'shot-gun' and I told him he was too small to sit in the front of the car. This upset did not start his day well. I then see if the students can identify with this story and ask them to show me how big their anger would be with their arms. Other stories include when Boris was trying to tie his shoelaces and got SO frustrated (introducing another word rather than just angry) and when Boris was competing in a race at the sports carnival and lost, and he felt disappointed and sad. Stories and emotions can be chosen to suit what is happening at school more generally so that one child does not feel targeted.

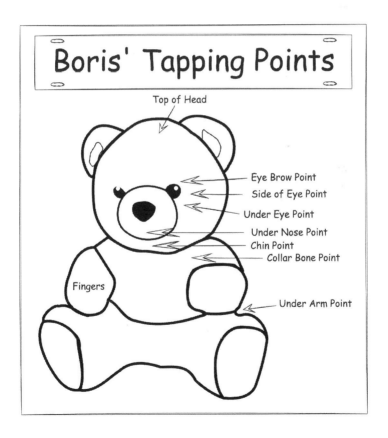

Boris' Tapping Points

Top of Head

Eye Brow Point
Side of Eye Point
Under Eye Point
Under Nose Point
Chin Point
Collar Bone Point

Fingers

Under Arm Point

While many mindfulness-based programs, such as Smiling Mind, support emotional regulation, we introduced tapping as it had an active component. Many young children struggle to sit or lie still and to keep their hands and feet to themselves during a quiet activity, and the focus on tapping helped with this. Tapping is easy to learn, and students can use it anywhere. No equipment or access to electricity or internet is needed. The time to do this is not much more than it takes to settle a class after a break, and the impact is much more significant.

Body percussion
Body percussion is a fun, easy-to-implement regulation activity. It can be very basic or more complex, dependent on the skills of those involved. It also uses rhythm to calm the amygdala. Diagrams with the primary rhythms are all that is needed to start. Some children can hold the instructions in their memory, but having pictorial visuals will ensure everyone can participate.

A simple example is:

Stomp, Stomp, Clap, Clap, Knee, Knee, Clap, Clap.
Stomp, Stomp, Clap, Clap, Knee, Knee, Clap, (Rest)
Clap, Clap, Knee, Knee, Clap, Knee, Clap, Knee.
Clap, Clap, Knee, Knee, Clap, Knee, Clap, (Rest)

The rhythm calms the amygdala, and the patterns connect the cortex as it takes thinking to coordinate the moves. Achieving rhythm together is calming; it creates a sense of connection and belonging that also benefits wellbeing. You can manipulate the volume and tempo to expend excess energy or to calm down.

Drumming
Many schools bought Djembe drums when someone had completed a drumming program, but then that staff member left, and the program could not continue. This situation is unfortunate, as there is much

research on the effectiveness of drumming as a means of stress reduction and emotional regulation. It may be helpful for schools to ensure they continue to have a staff member who can lead its implementation. Drumming is an accessible activity that students do not need extensive lessons to enjoy. As Varner states:

> *'The fun, physical nature of creating rhythmic sounds together is an activity that people are drawn to organically. Drumming together produces environments where people can experience the positive emotions of joy and social connectedness while reducing stress, tension, anxiety and depression.'* [93 (29)]

You can do many things with drums, but one activity to help regulation is playing fast and loud, then fast and soft, slow and loud and slow and gentle. Alternating between tempo and volume combinations takes concentration and impulse control. Another favourite activity is to start playing a rhythm on your drum, and then everyone plays one of the beats on their neighbour to the left's drum, back on their own and then to the right. This activity requires concentration and cooperation, and a willingness to make mistakes and accept others making them. It is also fun and builds connections within the group.

Clapping games

Handclapping games are an excellent activity for emotional regulation, providing rhythm, connection with one another and fun. They can also help build relationships on a more individual level if you ask a child to teach you a clapping game they know. If there are children from different cultures, there may be various games from their families. Some children may not have been exposed to these and may need to learn them. Mr Google and YouTube are your friends. Some versions include Miss Mary Mac, Rockin' Robin and Tic Tac Toe.

Mindfulness activities

Mindfulness is a practice where you have non-judgemental awareness of the present moment, not worrying about the past or the future. There are many ways to achieve this. You may focus on your breath, bodily sensations, or something external like music. Using programs like Smiling Mind is an easy way to introduce mindfulness to your classroom. They have a free app and recommend 10 minutes per day. There are also children's storybooks that can guide a mindfulness session.

Colouring or drawing mandalas can also be a mindfulness activity. Mandalas are circular and filled with geometric patterns. It is a peaceful and calming activity that focuses the mind. This can easily be incorporated as a regular activity.

Building with Lego, particularly without instructions, can be a mindful activity for children who struggle with this concept. You will notice that their focus will be just on what they are doing, and they will become totally absorbed.

Breathing activities

Many different breathing activities can make taking a slow deep breath fun! Buzzy bee breathing and rainbow breathing are great ways of breathing together as you can control the rate. Without this control, children will often take quick or shallow breaths. You want the child to extend their out-breath to get the greatest benefit. If doing it as a class, connecting with various students' gazes and smiling as you participate will give added benefits. We will cover these breathing activities more in the next chapter.

Yoga activities

Yoga also provides a way to assist with emotional regulation. Yoga increases body awareness and reduces stress.[94] While formal yoga practices are most effective, there is a benefit in introducing students to basic poses. There are many YouTube activities, stories and posters to aid the introduction of yoga to your class. Yoga dice and games that use yoga moves can increase engagement with these activities.

Music and movement

Music and movement activities are another fun way to practice regulation. It is likely that you already use a variety of music and movement breaks in your class, but did you know that their regular use can improve emotional regulation? You can again manipulate the tempo of the music to up-regulate or down-regulate your class. Sixty beats per minute are ideal for background music to maintain a calm environment. You can find playlists of these songs on music streaming sites.

> *'Music interventions are used for stress reduction in various settings because of the positive effects of music listening on physiological arousal (e.g. heart rate, blood pressure and hormonal levels) and psychological stress experiences (e.g. restlessness, anxiety and nervousness).'* [95]

Movement songs such as 'When All the Cows Were Sleeping', 'Row, Row, Row your Boat', 'The Wheels on the Bus' and 'Shake your Sillies Out' are excellent for younger students.

Role-play

Role-play can be an effective way of reinforcing strategies and the options available for self-regulation. It can help educate students about the boundaries of where you can go, how long you can stay and what you can do to help you regulate while there. Role-play can also be used to model different responses and their outcomes. This activity can be light-hearted and still be effective in establishing expectations. Stories are incredibly effective in educating.

Play

The value of play was discussed in the chapter about brain development. However, it is worth mentioning again in the context of activities that help children learn emotional regulation. Children naturally learn to manage impulses and regulate emotions through play, particularly pretend play and rough-and-tumble play with their peers. As children are exposed to fewer opportunities for play and are engaged in formal learning earlier, this natural process is shortened, potentially leaving them struggling to regulate their emotions and having difficulties with attention and focus.[96] Even giving older children the opportunity to play has many benefits.

Work and life skills

If your school has access to a garden, shovelling and raking provide students with patterned, repetitive movements combined with sensory integration. Both are useful for emotional regulation. If the activity is undertaken with an attentive and responsive adult, it will also be valuable for relationship-building. Baking can also be a sensory activity that aids regulation within the context of a relationship.

Preparing for storms

Even when these activities are performed regularly, there will still be times when a child will dysregulate in class. The next chapter will look at how to predict storms and implement strategies early; however, you need a disaster plan before even going to sea. All the crew need to know and understand the plan.

There must be an agreed, safe place for a child to go if they need time and space to calm their body and brain. It needs to be a place where adults will not interrogate the child for being out of class but will recognise that they are practising good self-regulation strategies by walking away and cooling down. A space within the classroom may facilitate this, or it may be in a specially created wellbeing space at the office, in the library or other suitable location. There may be regulation activities, such as fidgets, play dough, puzzles, mandalas to colour, etc. Teachers should establish rules around these spaces in the pre-sea training. Rules may include how long you can stay there, and a timer in the area may be helpful. However, if the student feels they are not yet ready to return, it may be worth allowing them to reset the timer and check in afterwards, as it can take some time for our nervous system to get back to pre-arousal levels.

Some teachers will recognise the importance of adding prevention activities to their daily routine and have the confidence to experiment. In contrast, others will find this outside their comfort zone and struggle to implement them even though they can see the benefit. If this is you, it may be worth discussing the situation with your colleagues. Maybe you can do joint class activities as you gain confidence. If time remains a barrier, it may be useful to note the time spent on behaviour management and diffusing emotional storms to get a realistic view of how much time prevention activities may free up. If things are working well for you and your students without changing anything, you are probably already doing an excellent job regulating and co-regulating your students.

Your challenge, should you choose to accept it, is ...

1. Choose an activity that you feel comfortable introducing to your class. *Ensure it is in your lesson plan so it is remembered.*

2. Commence doing it regularly.

3. Notice any changes and record them. When changes happen gradually, we often miss the impact.

CHAPTER 8

PREDICTING STORMS

Zoe's story: *Zoe started her day well. She likes coming to school. Zoe is in the 'safe and social' zone and ready to learn. She engaged well at the lesson's start and finished her work, but then started to wander and talk to a friend. The teacher had been dealing with other children's behaviour and did not realise that Zoe had finished. He gruffly told Zoe to 'sit down, be quiet and do her work'. Not an unusual direction in the classroom; however, the tone and abruptness of it triggered a flashback of the night before – of her stepfather yelling at and then hitting her mum.*

The flashback pushed her toward the 'fight or flight' zone. Zoe glared at the teacher, snapped that she had finished her work, but complied. Her muscles tightened, her heart beat faster, her breathing became more rapid and shallow, and her nervous system was hyper-alert for any other signs of danger. Then, Paul took her ruler without asking, pushing her further down the regulation ladder. She jumped up to chase Paul to claim back what was hers. Zoe has lost a lot in her short life, causing her to be sensitive about her belongings. The teacher reprimanded her sternly for being out of her seat, as this was the second time he had told her to sit down. Zoe is overwhelmed with the injustice of it all. She starts crying and then hides under a desk at the back of the classroom. They cannot coax her out. The report says that Zoe will not comply with instructions and becomes dysregulated when she is corrected.

Not all storms can be avoided, but managing a fully developed tornado takes much more time and energy than altering the course when a minor squall develops. Your experience and knowledge of the students in your class will mean you will be pretty good at predicting which students are more likely to dysregulate and in which situation, and which students have adequate coping skills and, if given time and space, will be able to self-manage.

If you notice a child when they are first starting to struggle and act purposefully to support them to stay in control, you can (mostly) avoid meltdowns. A child does not purposely lose control of their words and actions. It can be scary for them also. It is hard on their nervous system and damages their self-concept and relationships. There are also likely to be consequences afterwards that they would rather avoid. Noticing and responding to small changes in the weather will minimise disruptions to learning and allow the classroom's collective mood to stay positive and calm.

In the last chapter, we looked at whole-of-class strategies to undertake regularly to aid emotional regulation, and in this chapter, we will look at predicting storms and calming the seas. To predict storms, you need to be aware of the early signs of dysregulation and be able to quickly assess where the child is on the continuum of regulation. Are they still able to access the cognitive part of their brain and problem-solve, or are they stuck in their emotional brain and unable to respond to reason? You need to have all the adults in the classroom attuned to what is happening, and then, to calm the seas, you need to have a plan or a map that will guide everyone to respond consistently and compassionately.

> *'Students being unable to self-regulate frequently results in their behaviours being labelled as "naughty" or "challenging" by teachers. Continued dysregulation can lead to periods of suspension and exclusion, impacting both attendance rates for students and their broader families.'* [97]

The cost of not using strategies to minimise emotional storms that develop in your classroom is high. The highest cost is to your students. For some, it will result in suspension, some will be traumatised by the uncontrolled emotions of others, and all will miss out on learning. There is also a personal cost to your wellbeing. If a significant storm develops, it isn't easy to get the class back to baseline regulation, and you may find it challenging to regain your confidence, mood and composure. Teachers can also suffer from the effects of trauma after a significant incident. Early action is vital.

To be a good storm spotter, you must know what you are looking for and how a storm develops. Every person is unique with their own traumas, triggers and troubles, and how they react to these. So, you are looking for their body signs and reactions rather than what happened. What happened is important, especially when trying to resolve incidents between students, but things that will push one child into an emotional storm may not impact another student.

Window of tolerance

We all have a range where we can manage our emotions, a 'window of tolerance'.[19] If pushed outside this window, we may become either hypo-aroused or hyper-aroused. As mentioned in an earlier chapter, children with a trauma history, or those living with trauma, are likely to have a narrow window of tolerance. Hunger, worry about their family, tiredness, and other stressors will also narrow a child's window of tolerance. We have optimal functioning if we can stay within the window for much of the time. On a basic level, to predict storms, we are noticing if children are being pushed outside their window of tolerance, and we are offering the support needed to help them return to equilibrium.

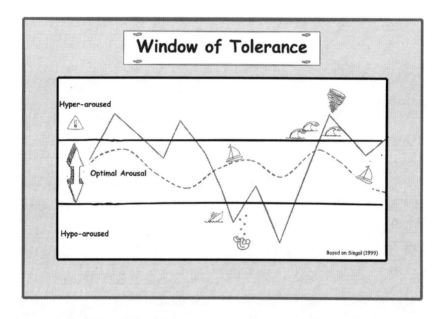

Polyvagal ladder

There are three primary autonomic nervous system states on the polyvagal ladder and some in-between and mixed states. However, the three primary states are most relevant to learning and emotional regulation. Deb Dana illustrates these on a ladder: safe and social at the top, fight and flight halfway down and freeze or shut down at the bottom.[4] As discussed earlier, we all have a default state that we go to when we are stressed. We go up and down the ladder many times a day, but if we can regulate, we can cope with these movements and not get stuck on one of the lower rungs.

While having different nuances, the window of tolerance and the polyvagal ladder are linked. They are both models to explain in understandable terms the very complex workings of our nervous systems. They also offer a way of recognising what is happening for both yourself and your students, which then provides an understanding of which strategies will work when.

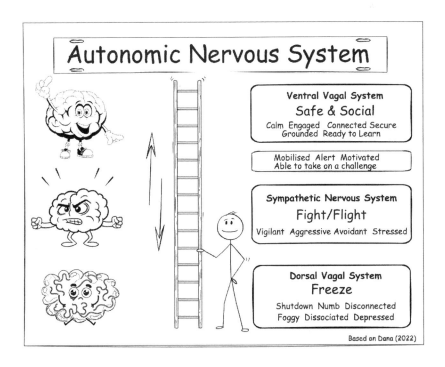

Fight or flight – Sympathetic nervous system

'Signs of dysregulation can be found on the face – wide eyes, looking around the room, looks of anger, surprise or disgust, body gestures, needing to move, perhaps pushing or hitting, etc. Those are signs of sympathetic nervous system activation.' [98]

The fight or flight state is familiar to many of us. When faced with what we perceive as a threat, we may feel the urge to get away from the situation (flight) or stay and fight or argue. We may not act on our urges due to our regulation skills, but we feel the impulse. People who internalise their emotions will likely resort to flight (or freeze). Those who externalise them are more likely to fight.

There are some situations where this state is essential for survival, but mostly, the classroom is not one of them. For a child, there may be situations where the fight or flight mode has kept them safe or helped them meet their needs. It has been an adaptive response. [89] The problem is that their nervous system may respond as if there is danger even though it is in a different environment.

Fight or flight is an automatic neural response to a perceived threat. It is not a chosen one. It is important to remember that it is about the danger that the nervous system *perceives* rather than any *actual* danger. If you asked the child afterwards, they might have no idea what triggered them initially. Once the autonomic nervous system is activated, it may only take a minor upset to cause them to dysregulate. Someone may 'look' at them or say something they interpret as derogatory, or the teacher may ask them to do something. A combination of things may have inadvertently added to the upset. If the child does identify a trigger, it is likely to be the last thing that happened – the straw that broke the camel's back – rather than the original 'threat' that the nervous system perceived.

When students run out of class or hide under their desks, they are in the flight state. The fight state is activated when they are hitting and yelling. Emotions connected with fight and flight include excitement, anger, frustration, annoyance, disgust, hate, stress, anxiety and fear.[73] Signs that may be noticeable include a wide alert gaze, fast, shallow breathing, rapid monotonous speech and a hunched posture. If the student could tune into their body, they might notice their heart beating fast and their muscles tense.[73] An interesting symptom is that while their hearing is hyper-alert for any sounds of danger, they may not hear what you say when in the fight or flight state. They are tuned into danger and survival.

Observable behaviours when a child is in fight or flight mode include moving around, yelling, intense crying, shaking, running away, social avoidance, attempts to dominate and control, aggression, lying and violence. Students with emotional regulation difficulties may often exhibit a combination of these behaviours.

Freeze, shut down – Dorsal nervous system

It's essential to look out for children who just shut down. Often these children get missed because their behaviour is less noticeable than those in fight or flight mode. Sometimes a child will go through 'fight or flight' to 'shut down'; however, for others, this will be their default position when stressed or overwhelmed. These children's behaviour does not tend to impact other students or teachers, so their distress may be inadvertently overlooked. These students are at risk of, or may already have, serious mental health concerns.

When a child is shutting down, they are likely to have glazed eyes and will tend to look down.[73] Their face may be blank, their mouth sad, and their body posture slumped.[73] They may wander slowly around with no real purpose, or they may freeze.[73] The child is likely to be quiet and make few sounds. If they do say anything, their voice will be flat and sad. They will disconnect and close others out of their world.[73]

Fawn

Fawn is not one of the autonomic states, but it is important to recognise these characteristics in a child. Fawn is a response characterised by a person responding to stress by trying to please and avoid conflict. This approach may have been an adaptive response to finding that the fight, flight or freeze responses did not bring safety or result in needs being met. This reaction is most common where the person has lived in an abusive situation. People-pleasing is often a trauma response.

Strategies to use early and regularly

Keeping a list of the strategies that might be useful in a particular situation can be helpful to you, others who provide support in your classroom and relief teachers. The previous chapter covered whole-of-class regulation activities; I cannot recommend highly enough to have these as regular parts of your day. However, some emotional storms may occur no matter what you do. Still, you can predict many of them through observation and minimise the fallout if your radar is attuned. It is helpful to ensure that all adults in your classroom have the knowledge and confidence to act if they notice any student starting to become stressed. Defusing may be as simple as 'being with' the student, verbally noticing that they are struggling with sitting still, for example. Acknowledge that sitting still can be challenging. Advise that standing and having a stretch may help. Model and encourage the child to reach as high as possible, lean to the left, lean to the right, put their hands down and stretch up again. Wriggle their shoulders to release tension. Take a big breath and then help them to re-engage.

Quick breathing strategies are an essential part of your everyday toolbox. They can be used as whole-of-class strategies and on an individual level. The more often students use breathing techniques, the more acceptable it will be for the child to use these early to prevent significant upsets. As mentioned in the last chapter, there are many different fun and engaging breathing strategies. This chapter includes more detailed instructions and the reasoning for using them.

Bumble bee breathing

- Breathe in slowly through your nose.
- Breathe out through your mouth, saying 'buzzzzzzzzzzz' for as long as you can.
- Repeat.

Young students particularly like it when you watch one another and compete with how long you can do the out-breath. When you are close to the end of your breath, go 'zip', signalling the end with your hands like you would with 'cut' for a movie.

Six reasons for doing something as simple as bumble bee breathing:

1. Slow, deep breaths calm the body and the brain, reducing blood pressure and slowing the heart rate.
2. The long out-breath resets the nervous system. The competition encourages them to lengthen it as long as possible.
3. It is playful – which creates a 'safe and social' environment.
4. Looking at one another builds a connection.
5. The fun and connection often induce a contagious smile, which improves mood, and 'feel good' hormones are released.
6. It also has a distraction function and moves the child from the emotional (fight or flight) part of the brain.

Snake breathing

- Breathe in slowly through your nose.
- Breathe out through your mouth, making a long, slow hissing sound.
- Repeat.

Again, with this one, you can see who can make the longest 'hisssss' and signal the end.

Hot chocolate breathing
- Pretend you are holding a steaming cup of hot chocolate.
- Breathe in deeply through your nose, smelling the delicious chocolate.
- Then breathe out through your mouth, pretending you are blowing the steam away.
- Repeat several times.

Rainbow breathing
- While breathing in, slowly put your arms up toward the sky.
- While breathing out, slowly bring your arms back to your side.
- Repeat.

Elephant breathing
- Put your two arms in front of you like a trunk.
- Lean over and suck up a trunk full of water as your hands go up above your head (breathing in through your nose).
- Blow out all the water (breathe out through your mouth) as your hands slowly go down to fill up again.

High five breathing
- Put your hand up in front of you with the palm facing you.
- Use your index finger of the other hand to trace up and down the fingers as you breathe.
- Breathe in as you go up your thumb and out as you go down.
- Then in as you go up your index finger and out as you go down.
- Continue for your whole hand.

It can be beneficial to ask which breathing activity a particular student likes or finds helpful. Having a choice of strategies and doing it in connection with someone else means they are more likely to agree to use one. It can fulfil their need for attention or connection and help regulate emotions by two paths. Familiarity with these strategies beforehand is essential. Having them on illustrated cards for the students to choose from can make them more inviting and provide them with a choice. Having a choice is an integral part of agency and empowerment.

Noticing that the child is moving from 'safe and social' to 'fight', 'flight' or 'freeze' is ideal. However, it is impossible to monitor every student constantly, so enlisting assistance is wise. Having teacher aids, or other adults in the classroom, on board to help monitor these changes is essential. It is also necessary for them to be aware of any plans and strategies you have in place and the freedom to suggest the child might like to go for a drink or do some colouring of a mandala. These simple strategies may stop minor upsets from developing further.

If Zoe could have been observed closely, someone might have seen the lead-up to her 'flight'. When she answered back, they may have been curious about her response and realised that she was no longer in a 'safe and social' space. Checking in calmly and compassionately may have changed her course down the ladder. Again, a teacher may not have had time to prioritise this, but maybe someone could. The other aspect is noticing that the tone and abruptness were the initial triggers at school. Monitoring how students are spoken to is important. However, we are all human and will not always get it right, and you need to be compassionate with yourself as well as with your students.

If several children are getting restless or you are getting overwhelmed, you can use your group regulation strategies. This approach can get everybody back onto a good level of regulation without singling out any one child. There's a place for both modes of action.

Some may still maintain that having strict behavioural rules and rigid expectations and consequences will solve any issues, but this approach disadvantages many children. Eventually, you want students to know when they are losing control and self-manage. However, this learning needs to be scaffolded. Some things a child needs to be able to self-manage are an awareness of what is happening in their body (interoception), an ability to identify their emotions and the emotions of others (emotional intelligence) and the ability to monitor their thoughts to control their behaviour.[97] We know that children who have experienced trauma, children with FASD or developmental delays and children with neurodiversity may take longer to develop these skills. Until they do, we need to observe, spot the storms and support them as required.

While recognising the difficulties of noticing the changing states of children, if time is not invested in diffusing the minor upsets in the classroom and a storm develops, it can take a long time to restore calm. The learning and wellbeing of the students will suffer. Like anything, storm spotting will get easier with practice. Using analogies, symbolism and stories adds to the playfulness of the process, which reduces your stress and positively influences the class. Humour must be used judiciously; however, it can be a powerful diffuser of building emotions when used well.

Your challenge, should you choose to accept it, is ...

1. Choose two students in your class and monitor their states. Notice when they are pushed outside their 'window of tolerance'.

2. Be curious about what happened and why?

3. Try responding by supporting them to regulate.

CHAPTER 9

DISTRIBUTE
THE LIFE RAFTS

Felix's story: *Felix is in Year 8. His morning has started badly. He came to school out of sorts, and things have not improved. He is restless and keeps walking around. The teacher directed him to sit down and do his work three times. Felix is getting more agitated and defiant and is nearing getting his name put on the board to stay in at lunchtime to complete his*

work. And then, the teacher is in disbelief as he asks to go and get a drink!
He is told a definite 'no'! His teacher firmly tells him that he has not done
anything all morning and cannot waste more time by going for a drink.
Felix managed to stay in the classroom for another 15 minutes but could
not focus and was hyper-alert for any further threat – and he found it.
A student 'looked' at him. He hit the student, and it all went downhill.

We've discussed whole-of-class prevention strategies, and individual or whole-of-class activities to diffuse minor upsets. If emotions escalate above this level, you must actively provide a life raft to the individual student to prevent further escalation and intense emotional storms. This action to control and regulate the mood in the classroom will protect your wellbeing and ability to teach and manage the class effectively.[99] Extreme emotional outbursts increase stress, anxiety and emotional fatigue. It can lead to burnout, so avoiding them is not only in the student's interest but also yours. By providing a life raft, you are also protecting the wellbeing of the rest of your students and reducing the valuable teaching time needed to attend to the fallout in the aftermath of explosions. You also provide a compassionate response to the child and meet their immediate needs.

While mental health professionals focus on the link between behaviour and emotions, schools and teachers often focus on behavioural management. This focus on behaviour can mean the need it is communicating is missed. Punitive responses to the behaviour are not helpful.

> *'It's often thought a tough approach to behaviour is the way forward*
> *for schools. But research shows that punitive responses, such as*
> *writing names on the board, taking away a student's lunchtime,*
> *or handing out detention, are actually ineffective in the long term*
> *and can exacerbate student disengagement and alienation.'*[100]

There is often a brief time window where it is possible to divert the storm and prevent a full-blown crisis. If the storm is diverted, the available learning time for students is increased and the wellbeing of you and your class is protected. You also protect the child from the unpleasant experience of being out of control. If they are not supported to regulate, particularly if they have asked to use a regulation strategy and the request was refused, you must consider whether or not the responsibility for the outcome lies entirely with the student. If the school has steadfast rules around children not being out of class during lesson time, preventing the use of regulation strategies such as getting a drink or going outside and having time and space to regulate, the system also holds responsibility. It is so much better for a child to be able to go outside to an agreed area for an agreed time than to have them run off when they become dysregulated. This situation presents a serious safety issue and often involves several staff members trying to locate and contain the child. Boundaries are needed, but flexibility and adaptability are also required.

There are many strategies to use when an emotional storm is pending. Their effectiveness will depend on the individual child and the situation and how far down the regulation ladder they have gone before intervention occurs or is possible. Providing a life raft can be as simple as offering a choice of activities within your boundaries.

STOP
DON'T DO ANYTHING
TAKE A BREATH
SLOW AND DEEP
OBSERVE
WHAT IS HAPPENING
PLAN
ACTION THAT WON'T MAKE THINGS WORSE

The STOP Strategy

The STOP Strategy is helpful for teachers and all students. I have found this strategy useful for both children and adults, with some adults telling me that they have found it helpful in preventing violence in their homes when both persons are committed to change. It is an effective and accessible strategy for everyone. It is beneficial for a teacher to use before they engage with an escalating student, and it is a valuable skill to teach students. Self-regulation requires us to pause between our feelings and actions; this approach will help achieve that.

Stop, step back.

- When someone dysregulates, they need their space. They also need demands to stop, as placing further demands on them will mean they will retreat further into the emotional part of the brain where their options are fight or flight – or shut down. Trying to reason with a dysregulated child or adult will not work.
- I also include 'stop moving' for students to keep their hands and feet still.

Take a breath.

- Slightly exaggerate your calming breath as the student's mirror neurons will likely fire with yours. Unless they have practised taking slow, deep breaths, or you have a strong, trusting relationship with them, telling them to take a breath may not be helpful. The daily practice of these strategies means that they are available when needed.

Observe what is happening.

- Observe your thoughts and feelings.
- Observe your muscle tension and posture.

- Consciously relax and soften your stance.
- Observe your tone of voice.
- Observe, are they pressing your buttons? And, in turn, are you pushing theirs? You are human, and when there are heightened emotions, this happens. If we notice it, we can do something about it.

Plan – Plan helpful action. Another way of looking at this is to do something that won't worsen the situation because sometimes that is all we can do. Acting rather than reacting is critical. The more often we do this, the better we become at it.

Helpful actions include:

- Giving a choice but maintaining boundaries
- Name it to tame it
- Give space (time and physical)
- Provide an activity that will either soothe and calm or distract.

Get a drink

Any easy, and usually first option, is to suggest they go for a walk and get a drink of water. This approach works in a few ways.

- It gives both the student and teacher some time and space to regulate.
- Walking can lower their level of arousal and stress hormone levels.
- It can be a distraction from what was causing distress.
- It can remove them from the triggering event or environment.
- If they splash cold water on their face, it can help reset the autonomic nervous system.

Sensory activities

Sensory needs vary with each individual. A child may have known sensory needs that we should aim to meet regularly, and especially when they have heightened emotions. Others may not have identified needs but will find using such things as play dough or kinetic sand calming. Stress balls and fidgets can also be helpful and may be something you would have in your calming space. It is best to establish the rules around sensory activities before they are introduced and non-confrontationally reinforce these rules when the child is experiencing heightened emotions.

Cognitive activities

If a child is not too far down the regulation ladder, distraction activities that can move them from their emotional brain to their thinking brain can be helpful. This distraction may be a game of Connect Four, UNO or even Snap. These activities also assist by removing demands but maintaining the relationship. There is no demand to talk or problem-solve now; just play the game. Noughts and Crosses is another practical activity in this context, as we can play it anywhere. You can even use a stick and draw the game in the dirt. A teacher aide may take responsibility for assisting children in this way when required. Having a separate space for these individual regulation activities may be beneficial to limit distractions to other students.

Heavy work activity

You can organise this activity when planning for emotional regulation in your classroom. If using this strategy, it is essential to implement it before the student is at the point of no return. You need to pre-arrange with a colleague to go along with what may seem like a strange errand. Ask the child to take a reasonably heavy pile of books or resources to another teacher's classroom for you. Include a brief note. The receiving teacher thanks the child for their helpfulness. By using this strategy, you have given the child the time and space to regulate, and the walk and using their big muscles will also help with regulation. You have given yourself the space to regulate and maintain your relationship with the student. The student feels needed and helpful and receives positive reinforcement.

Felix's story

Consider how things could have been different for Felix. At what point could the teacher or another adult have intervened in this process?

There are a few points where the proponents could have altered the course of events: the teacher could have first noticed that he was sad or upset and 'named it to tame it'.[74] This simple intervention can have an incredible effect. Even if you get it wrong, they will likely correct you and say how they feel. Knowing that you notice them and 'get' them is incredibly powerful. Then the teacher or teacher aide could have noticed that they were restless – and again named it to tame it. As this was a step further down the regulation ladder, they could have also asked them what they might find helpful to settle – going for a drink, maybe doing a few deep breaths or some tapping if this is something he was used to doing. A staff member could have offered Felix a game of Connect Four or asked him to go on an errand. The connection gained by being shown care will help calm them and make it more likely that they will sit down when they return to class. It may not be magic – as the distress they are feeling may be more profound than a brief intervention can solve. The last point where there may have been a successful diversion of the storm was when the young person asked to go for a drink. He may have just wanted to get out of the classroom, but if we are curious, the question is then, why? He may not have wanted to do his work. If this is the case, wondering why may give us some insight into his needs.

Providing students with a 'life raft' when they are nearing an emotional storm is one of the most contentious issues for some teachers. With more knowledge, beliefs are changing. However, many still believe that meeting the regulation needs of a child is giving in and rewarding bad behaviour, when in fact, if given early, it can avoid 'bad behaviour', that is, behaviour that results from dysregulation. You must consider your reasons for not meeting these needs and whether your approach is proving effective and in line with current research. Children need consistent boundaries to feel safe; however, they must be regulated to make good decisions. The best thing we can do to help them make good decisions is to support their regulation early.

Your challenge, should you choose to accept it, is …

1. Choose strategies that are within your comfort zone and fit within your boundaries. Discuss these with the other adults in your class.

2. Educate your students about equity and equality. Different children need different things to support their education. Children need to learn about people having different needs from an early age to avoid perpetuating the marginalisation of difference.

3. Try distributing life rafts as needed.

CHAPTER 10

RIDE THE WAVES

Felix's story continued: *After hitting the other student, Felix ran out of the classroom. A teacher's aide, Jo, followed him at a distance to give him space and to ensure his safety. A teacher walks by. They are unaware of what has led him to be there, and they try to convince Felix to return to class. Felix's anger again escalates. The teacher remains calm and tries to reason with Felix – explaining the consequences of not complying and continuing to try and get him back to class. The teacher's aide did not intervene as she did not want to challenge the teacher's authority.*

Sometimes, storms will quickly build, no matter what you do. Your prevention and early intervention activities will minimise the frequency, but sometimes, you must ride the waves. Instead of trying to calm the storm, you must wait for it to pass. You will not antagonise the situation if you focus on riding the waves and ensuring safety, and you are less likely to take the child's behavioural response to their emotions personally.

If staff have a shared narrative about where on the regulation ladder the child is, they can easily communicate this to one another. One can say, 'We are riding the waves' rather than giving a detailed account of what happened, which can cause further upset, particularly if your account does not fit the child's perspective. Staff would then have a shared understanding of what actions (or inactions) will support the child and the person helping them. Riding the waves fits with neuroscientific ways of regulating emotions.

> *'People who struggle with overwhelming emotions often feel vulnerable. At any point, the slightest trigger can lead to a tidal wave of emotions, leaving them feeling confused, angry, alone, hopeless and in pain.'*[101]

During this time, they must know that you are there for them but do not make demands or invade their space unless your relationship with them allows this. Storms always pass. They will pass quicker if you do not fuel the fire.

If you persist with demanding compliance and explanations of behaviour, they are likely to dysregulate further, leading to more severe reactions and consequences. What was the original problem will be overshadowed by the behaviours that occur as the child escalates. If we push the child into these behaviours rather than providing them with the time, space and support to regulate, we hold some responsibility for the outcome.

Dr Bruce Perry provides a neuro-sequential model to use when riding the waves. The 3 Rs Model is Regulate, Relate and Reason. You must first assist the student in regulating: to calm their fight and flight response. You need to ensure they feel physically and emotionally safe. Once they are regulated, you must re-establish your relationship – and then, finally, you can reason, find out what happened, and discuss learnings and consequences. You mustn't rush to this final stage; emotions can quickly escalate again if they remain heightened.

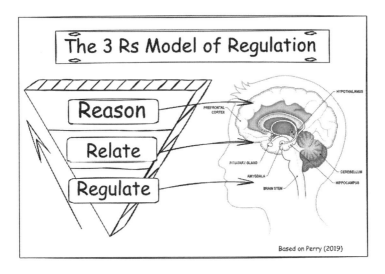

Based on Perry (2019)

Felix is now in full 'fight or flight' mode, with his body reacting to what it interprets as imminent danger. Remember, it is an automatic response to a neuroception of danger, an assessment outside Felix's conscious awareness. His sympathetic nervous system is activated. A sudden release of hormones has triggered this system to stimulate the adrenal and pituitary glands, which release adrenaline, noradrenaline and cortisol.[102]

His heart is beating faster, his blood pressure has risen, and his breathing is rapid and shallow. His muscles are tensed and ready to either defend himself or run away. His response system has diverted blood away from his skin and digestive system, toward his muscles, brain, legs and arms. His pupils are dilated to give him a greater awareness of his immediate surroundings.

As you can see, telling Felix to calm down will not be effective in the face of this biological response. It can take Felix's parasympathetic system twenty to sixty minutes to get back to the baseline *after* the threat has gone. If we go in too soon to try to reason, we are likely to prolong the process. Your observations, knowledge of your students and your existing trusting relationship will put you in the best position to judge when you can try to reconnect and when you need to step back.

Once the teacher had stepped away from Felix, Jo could explain the situation. The teacher left Jo to monitor from a distance. Felix eventually sat down in the eating area.

Fred's story: *Fred is in prep. He finds it hard to sit at his desk and do the activities his classmates are doing. He wanders around, and the teacher encourages him to sit and do the activity. It appears Fred is in his own little world and either ignores or does not register this instruction. The teacher more firmly tells him to sit down and do his work. Fred starts crying quietly and hides under a desk. The teacher gives him time and space and instructs other students to leave him. After a while, the teacher encourages Fred to come out and do the activity. Fred is no longer crying but shakes his head in refusal and remains under the desk. The teacher tells him that he will not be able to play at morning tea time if he has not done his work – and returns to teaching the class. Fred does eventually come out but does not want to join his peers. He sat to eat his morning tea but was not allowed to play during the break. His day did not improve, and he soon gained a reputation for being a non-compliant child.*

Even though Fred's version of 'flight or fight' (or perhaps even shut down) is much quieter and has less impact on others, the emotional experience may be just as great or greater than the child who yells, shouts and runs out of the room. You may have been able to prevent this situation with your skills and knowledge; however, if it has reached the point where you need to ride the waves, it is essential to remember the 3Rs to get him back on track and maintain the relationship. Due to human tendencies, this situation will often become a battle of wills. Rather than keeping our eye on the destination, we get stuck in the storm and struggle for power. In times of stress, we often revert to 'power over' rather than 'power with' the students.

In the 'riding the waves' period, you aim to regulate. To achieve this state, you need to take away all demands. This approach is not taking away their responsibility; however, attempting to reason at this stage will be futile as that part of the brain will not be responsive. After achieving regulation and the relationship is re-established, there will be time to reason.

'Naming it to tame it' can be helpful so the child knows you understand their feelings. Again, this approach is not condoning their actions but understanding the big emotion. 'Being there' is important. Careful judgement of what this means is necessary. For some, it will be staying near them; for others, it will require giving them space. We need them to return to their biological baseline. They are already outside their window of tolerance, and it will be counterproductive to push them further out. The threat of removing such things as playtime in response to emotional reactions overwhelming the child will not aid regulation. It is essential to note that play increases the development of regulation skills, so removing access to it, may not provide the desired outcome.

Your challenge, should you choose to accept it, is …

1. Experiment with 'riding the waves'.

2. Notice your feelings when you do this. It can be challenging, and it can take courage to shift approaches.

3. Notice how many storms occurred this week. Keep a record of change.

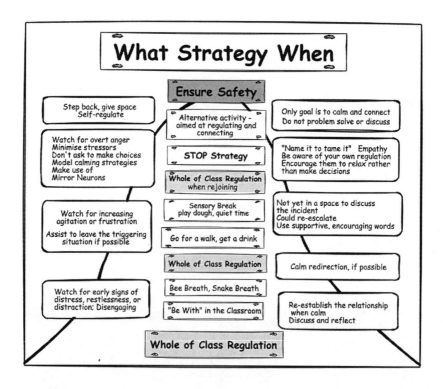

What Strategy When

Ensure Safety

Step back, give space
Self-regulate

Watch for overt anger
Minimise stressors
Don't ask to make choices
Model calming strategies
Make use of
Mirror Neurons

Watch for increasing
agitation or frustration

Assist to leave the triggering
situation if possible

Watch for early signs of
distress, restlessness, or
distraction: Disengaging

Alternative activity -
aimed at regulating and
connecting

STOP Strategy

Whole of Class Regulation
when rejoining

Sensory Break
play dough, quiet time

Go for a walk, get a drink

Whole of Class Regulation

Bee Breath, Snake Breath

"Be With" in the Classroom

Only goal is to calm and connect
Do not problem solve or discuss

"Name it to tame it" Empathy
Be aware of your own regulation
Encourage them to relax rather
than make decisions

Not yet in a space to discuss
the incident
Could re-escalate
Use supportive, encouraging words

Calm redirection, if possible

Re-establish the relationship
when calm
Discuss and reflect

Whole of Class Regulation

CHAPTER 11

AFTER THE STORM

Felix's story continued: *After giving him some more time, Jo went and asked Felix if she could sit there too. Felix agreed. He was calm enough to tolerate the presence of a supportive adult. Jo knew the situation could escalate again if she asked him 'why'. She sat a while and then asked if he would like a game of Noughts and Crosses, which they played with chalk on the concrete where they were sitting. Jo anticipated that this game would help Felix reconnect with the cognitive (thinking) part of his brain rather than him staying stuck in his emotions. She also thought that it would help repair the relationship. She then asked him if he would like to go and get a drink and wash his face with cold water (this can reset the vagal nervous system), and then they would return to class and check out what the class was up to.*

After the storm has passed, and it always passes, the next steps of the 3Rs approach, Relate and Reason, need to be followed. If you take this approach, the crisis will resolve more quickly and have fewer long-term impacts on the students and yourself. The whole class will be able to return to the pre-crisis state more quickly, and the neuroception of safety you have fostered with them will have minimal disruption. Managing the aftermath of emotional storms in this way ensures the skills of relationship repair are actively modelled, providing students with a template for life. The student will be less likely to internalise that they are 'bad' but understand that they may need to gain the skills required to manage the situation. Understanding that the outcome results from a skills deficit provides a way forward as we can teach the necessary skills. Using an approach based on brain science offers a predictable way to move from a crisis back to effective teaching and learning, which is the overarching aim of the process within a school context. In times of high stress, having a simple and effective formula to guide our actions proactively is helpful, as our cognitive functions may not be at peak functioning.

> *'Dr Bruce Perry, a pioneering neuroscientist in the field of trauma, has shown us that to help a vulnerable child to learn, think and reflect, we need to support them in a sequence that prioritises regulation first so that the brainstem can be calmed. Heading straight for the "reasoning" part of the brain with an expectation of learning will not work so well if the child is dysregulated and disconnected from others.'* [103]

Failure to focus on repairing the relationship after the storm has settled may result in tensions remaining between the teacher and the student, which will mean that both parties may remain close to the edges of their window of tolerance. It will take little to push either of them outside of this zone again. The tension is palpable and reduces the neuroception of safety necessary for learning. If the reconnection does not occur positively, the student may revert to making bids for connection in less productive ways. As highlighted earlier, students will seek any attention to meet their need for connection, including the negative attention gained by acting out.

It is not only the student's regulation that you need to monitor. It is essential to ensure your regulation is close to its baseline before doing anything else. If you need additional time before repairing the relationship, it is okay to say that you need time and space. It is important to be authentic.

Damaged relationships can be repaired in many ways: a relational game, shared experiences, verbal and non-verbal communication, or gentle humour if the pre-existing relationship allows this. Verbal communication may be acknowledging that you know it was tough for them. Games such as Connect Four, SPOT It and Noughts and Crosses have the potential for intermittent non-stressful conversation, light-hearted competition and fun – and require the involvement of the cognitive parts of our brains.

Repair may happen quickly, or it may need time and space to occur, depending on the strength of the previous relationship and the damage done by words and actions during the emotional storm. The aim at this point is re-establishing the relationship rather than getting the student to apologise or accept responsibility and consequences. Students who have had ruptures and repairs to relationships from their earliest years will generally cope with this well. However, those without lots of modelling of this process may struggle and doubt that they can return from a damaged relationship.

'If kids come to us from strong, healthy, functioning families, it makes our job easier. If they do not come to us from strong, healthy, functioning families, it makes our job more important.'[104]

After relationship repair, the focus can move to 'reasoning'. However, knowing the desired outcome is essential before reasoning with the child. Is it about identifying the skill deficit so you can explicitly teach it, getting the child to accept responsibility and apologise, or assisting the child to gain insight into their behaviours? Is it about punishment, natural consequences or restorative justice? The focus of the reasoning step will depend on what the system dictates and the teacher's values and beliefs. Reflecting on this aspect of the process will guide the teacher in the conversation. Lecturing does not tend to change behaviour, and listening with an open heart to the child's perception of events is essential. There are often bits of what happened that you may have missed – or have misinterpreted. Often systems and the behaviour of others have contributed to the situation, and this needs to be acknowledged. Being open to apologising (if appropriate) for your part in the event models values and behaviour that are important to the child's development.

'When we apologise and repair, we teach our kids how to make amends when they make mistakes in relationships.'[105]

If identifying skill deficits, barriers to using established skills, and restorative justice are the aim of the conversation, content may include:

- Tell me about what happened. I was worried about you.
- Was there a place where you (or someone else) could have done something differently?
- Is there a strategy that may have been useful in this situation?
- Was there something that made it difficult for you to do this?
- Can we role-play an alternative story – and an alternative ending?
- These are some other strategies that others find helpful. Is there an extra one that sounds useful to you?

- Do you need to do something to help make this right with the other person?

If the focus includes previously advised or natural consequences, including this in the conversation is relatively easy. It is essential to be matter-of-fact and that your approach indicates that you intend for it to be a learning experience with them accepting responsibility for *their* role in the incident. It is also necessary to understand their stage of emotional development, have empathy for their feelings and recognise the contributing factors or other people's roles in the incident. Children have a strong sense of justice which can override all other reasoning.

> *Developing caring and empathy in children is best done by modelling caring and concern toward the child.*[106]

Some questions that may be useful if the intention is for the student to gain insight into their behavioural response include:

- What led to the situation?
- How did you interpret what happened?
- What was said?
- How intense were your emotions? (0–100)
- Did your emotions influence the other person/s actions or what they said? If yes, how? Did your emotions affect your actions? If yes, how?
- Did your emotions influence your judgement? If yes, how?[107]

In teaching situations, a teacher is unlikely to be able to do this work immediately and will depend on teacher aides, behaviour specialists and administration staff to support this approach. Whoever's role has been to monitor the student's safety while they calm down outside the classroom often takes the lead in this. This whole-of-staff approach reinforces the value of everyone being on the same page in supporting children's emotional regulation. If the person managing the student is angry or frustrated with the student or the situation, it would not be a good time to try and re-establish the relationship. It would be preferable if another person could step in and maintain the status quo until both parties are regulated.

Relationship repair may also be necessary between students. Sometimes these relationships have already been repaired by students in their own time and space. By the time adults can facilitate this or try to enforce an apology, the students may be long past this point in their processing. This is always worth checking to avoid reigniting fires.

'Education … is painful, continual and difficult work to be done in kindness, by watching, by warning, by praise, but above all, by example.' [108]

Your challenge, should you choose to accept it, is ...

1. Try using this three-stage approach in minor incidents to gain confidence in the outcomes.

2. Consciously leave reasoning until the child has regulated and relationship repair has occurred. This theory makes sense, but it can take much work to implement as we all tend to resort to trying to use logic early.

3. Consider the impact the system had on the crisis, the impact of school rules, the effect of staff actions and the impact of the child's behaviour. How could the incident have been prevented – or minimised?

CHAPTER 12

REVIEWING THE LOGBOOK AND MAPPING THE FUTURE

Let's return to Riley's story, six months later:

It is a Friday morning at the end of the term. Again, Riley is tired, but over the last six months, he has made a conscious effort to look after his wellbeing. He acknowledges he has lapses in his endeavours, but he generally eats well and does some exercise. Riley has also learnt to have some self-compassion and realises that beating himself up over failures is not productive and can add to his stress. He is more self-aware and has implemented strategies in his classroom that, while experimental at first, have seen some positive changes as they have become more established practices.

It is Friday morning. I am exhausted. It has been another long term. Most students are doing their work, but Jordan is restless, wandering around and annoying others. Over time I have gotten to know Jordan better, and he often seems this way when he has had a hard time at home. What may have happened this morning or last night for him? He seemed all right yesterday. I check in with him and ask him if he is okay. His response is abrupt and gruff. I notice my jaw tense in response to his reply. I expected my concern to be met with more equanimity. I use the STOP strategy for my own regulation and consider whether a whole-of-class regulation activity may be helpful – or whether an individual approach would be better at this stage. He seemed pretty upset, so I went straight for 'naming it to tame it' and then offering a life raft. I acknowledged that he seemed angry and unsettled this morning and offered a choice of life raft: to go for a walk and get a drink or spend ten minutes colouring a mandala. He chose to go for a drink, and when he returned, I commenced a brief tapping session with the whole class. The class is now quite used to us having both regular and random (responsive) tapping sessions, so no-one questioned what was happening. The whole class, including Jordan, returned to their work after we had finished. I reflected on how different the outcome was this term.

If nothing changes, nothing changes. Emotional storms are common in classrooms today and negatively impact teaching, learning, and student and staff wellbeing. While acknowledging the difficulties in implementing change and the courage required, change is essential to achieve different outcomes. A calmer classroom is dependent on attitudes, actions and approaches that aim to support this way of being. A more peaceful classroom will mean that you will enjoy your role more, students will enjoy coming to your lessons and relationships will improve. This process has a cyclic effect. All the areas are interdependent and cumulative and will significantly affect your students' experience of education.

If we mindlessly continue doing things the way we have always done, we will reproduce past errors, and the same issues will continue. Children will not have their learning or emotional needs met, and teachers will continue to suffer significant stress and burnout. There has to be a better way.

Have you accepted the challenges proposed at the end of each chapter, and if you have, what changes have you noticed? Changes happen gradually; unless we take time to reflect, we miss them and settle into the new normal. Did you start making changes and revert to the old ways of doing things in times of stress? This process is an entirely human response. The Stages of Change Model shows how cyclic it is.[109] The stages include denial or lack of recognition of the problem, contemplating, preparing for change, and finally, actively enacting change.[109] Once a person has achieved the desired outcome, maintenance follows. However, it rarely happens in a straight line and relapsing and reverting to old ways may occur at any stage. It is then possible to re-join the cycle where you diverted, or at an earlier stage if that better fits where you are. It is a process that can take many attempts. The important thing is starting – and then, if a relapse occurs, you take stock and start again.

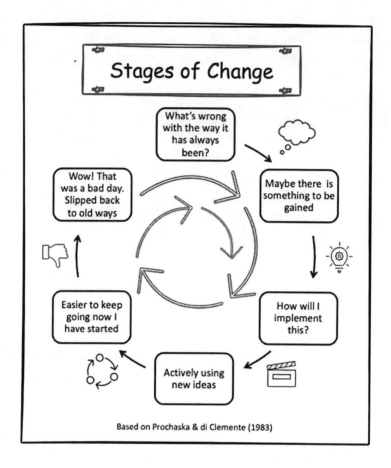

Stages of Change

What's wrong with the way it has always been?

Maybe there is something to be gained

How will I implement this?

Actively using new ideas

Easier to keep going now I have started

Wow! That was a bad day. Slipped back to old ways

Based on Prochaska & di Clemente (1983)

Reflecting on the journey

While *Emotional Storms* has provided additional ideas and resources, it is not a magic wand. Many systems, community and personal issues impact our ability to implement change. When we are stressed or overwhelmed, our access to our internal resources is limited. It also takes significant courage to change in an environment where most people accept the status quo.

I have posed the following questions to aid reflection on the journey you have taken through the chapters of this book. Often, we think we don't have time for reflection, but it is an essential part of learning and change. We need to reflect on where we have come from and what we have learnt to plan our next adventures successfully.

I hope you have identified and enacted strategies for your self-care. If you have only achieved this step, it will have improved the wellbeing of yourself and your students. You make an incredible difference in the life of students, and to continue doing this and prevent burnout, you need self-care. Your wellbeing is so essential. It is the anchor for all other strategies. Without this grounding, things will eventually go adrift. Put on your life jacket first and maintain those activities and connections that help you to thrive.

With additional information and insights, are you more curious about behaviours? When a child is displaying unwanted behaviours, do you wonder why? Remember, there may be reasons associated with their stage of development, neurodiversity or life experiences that impact their behaviour. Are they expressing unmet needs? Or are they lacking the required skills? Curiosity about the causes of behaviours leads to us responding with more compassion.

Have connections between yourself and your students improved? Learning occurs in a positive and supportive relationship, so achieving these connections is vital. Are you more aware of your student's strengths – particularly the non-academic strengths of your students who struggle? Have you been able to introduce an activity to your plan for the day that aims to reduce stress and maintain (or regain) regulation for the entire class? Did you find an activity you are comfortable with doing consistently? If you have achieved this – congratulations! The difference you have made can last a lifetime!

Are you able to consciously provide experiences of co-regulation for students when it is required? Can you share your calm rather than join their storm? When reflecting on students' coping skills and the strategies they use, have these improved? Are they using them effectively? And have the barriers to students using these when needed been reduced?

Have you noticed how you influence the weather and actively worked on producing sunnier days? Are you more aware of your body language, your vocal tone and the power of a smile? These are simple strategies but are potent ways to set the tone of the classroom.

Have you become an expert storm spotter? The skill of identifying where a child is on the ladder of regulation and teaching them to use regulation strategies early, before a storm emerges, will not only make for a calmer classroom but will have ongoing benefits for your students.

Have the 3Rs (regulate, relate, reason) become an essential part of your toolbox, a go-to strategy when you need to ride the waves? This neuroscience-based approach can prevent you from inadvertently prolonging the storm by trying to reason with or make demands upon a dysregulated child.

Remember, it's not possible to have all the answers or all the strategies. Despite your best efforts, students will sometimes dysregulate, and you will become dysregulated, too. No strategy is magic. They work some of the time. However, the bigger your toolbox, the better equipped you are. An understanding of brain development and the states of regulation can help you be more effective more of the time. You will find you already have strategies that work, so use these. Some of your existing classroom strategies may align with those in this book or have slight variations. I hope this book has reinforced your continued use of them and increased your understanding of why they work.

Some of the strategies may appear like you are rewarding 'bad' behaviour. However, what you are doing is helping the child to return to a regulated place where they can reflect and learn. Remember, a child cannot think logically when that part of their brain is disconnected due to an emotional storm.

Many of the ideas may be new as they link the knowledge of child development and the counselling world with the world of the classroom. Implementing multiple new things in your life and classroom can be overwhelming. If you have not been as successful as you would like as you have progressed through this book, it would be helpful to establish *one* SMART goal (see Chapter 1). You may want to start with a goal associated with self-care, an awareness of body language or introducing a regulation strategy to your class. Or you could initially focus on the high end of emotional regulation and practice using the 3Rs. Go back to any of these chapters and let one idea that clicks with you be the focus of your goal. Even changing one thing will make a difference.

As you continue your journey, remember that:

- Your wellbeing is the number one priority
- Any change you implement will make a difference
- Change may take time to be apparent
- One safe and significant person in a vulnerable child's life makes a difference
- Teaching students to stay regulated is much easier than calming a dysregulated child
- Prevention is key
- Be curious. Be compassionate. Be kind – to yourself as well as your students.

I wish you fair winds and following seas.

Your challenge, should you choose to accept it, is ...

1. Document what you have implemented.

2. Document changes.

3. Celebrate successes – even small ones.

REFLECTION:
WHERE ARE YOU NOW?

HOW DO YOU RATE YOUR:

Self-care ★★★★★

Knowledge of Childhood Development ★★★★★

Knowledge of Trauma and ACEs ★★★★★

Ability to Self-Regulate ★★★★★

Knowledge of Neurodiversity ★★★★★

Connection with your students ★★★★★

Knowledge of Emotional Regulation ★★★★★

Use of Prevention Strategies ★★★★★

Confidence to deal with Emotional Storms ★★★★★

Date:

REFERENCES

1. Taney AM. *The Challenge of Promoting the Well-being of Young People in High School: The Perspective of Teachers*. Honours thesis. James Cook University; 2006.

2. Heffernan A, Longmuir F, Bright D, Kim M. *Perceptions of teachers and teaching in Australia*. 2019. Accessed February 10, 2023. https://www.monash.edu/thank-your-teacher/docs/Perceptions-of-Teachers-and-Teaching-in-Australia-report-Nov-2019.pdf

3. Felitti VJ, Anda RF, Nordenberg D, et al. Relationship of childhood abuse and household dysfunction to many of the leading causes of death in adults. The Adverse Childhood Experiences (ACE) Study. *American Journal of Preventive Medicine*. 1998;14(4):245–258. doi:10.1016/s0749-3797(98)00017-8

4. Dana D. *Polyvagal Theory in Therapy: Engaging the Rhythm of Regulation*. W W Norton & Company; 2018.

5. Carroll A, Forrest K, Sanders-O'Connor E, et al. Teacher stress and burnout in Australia: examining the role of intrapersonal and environmental factors. *Social Psychology of Education*. 2022;(25):441–469. doi:10.1007/s11218-022-09686-7

6. Brost A. 200 Self-care quotes to remind you to take care of you! The Derm Review. n.d. Accessed January 20, 2023. https://thedermreview.com/self-care-quotes/

7. Life in Mind. A guide to self care. 2023. Accessed March 1, 2023. https://lifeinmind.org.au/research/self-care

8. Pollan M. *In Defence of Food: An Eater's Manifesto*. Penguin Books; 2009.

9. National Health and Medical Research Council. The Australian guide to healthy eating. Australian Government. 2023. Accessed March 1, 2023. https://www.eatforhealth.gov.au/guidelines/australian-guide-healthy-eating

10. World Health Organisation. Physical activity. World Health Organisation. n.d. Accessed February 25, 2023. https://www.who.int/news-room/fact-sheets/detail/physical-activity

11. Hirshkowitz M, Whiton K, Albert SM, et al. National Sleep Foundation's sleep time duration recommendations: methodology and results summary. *Sleep Health*. 2015;1(1):40–43. doi:10.1016/j.sleh.2014.12.010

12. Brigham and Women's Hospital. Light-emitting e-readers before bedtime can adversely impact sleep. n.d. Accessed April 27, 2023. https://www.brighamandwomens.org/about-bwh/newsroom/press-releases-detail?id=1962

13. Harris R. *The Happiness Trap: Stop Struggling, Start Living*. Exisle Publishing Limited; 2007.

14. Baxter LP, Gardner F, Southall AE. Reflecting on teaching in low SES areas during COVID-19: an Australian experience. *Cambridge Journal of Education*. 2022;53(2)177–193. doi:10.1080/0305764x.2022.2092071

15. McLuhan M. Quoteslyfe. n.d. Accessed March 23, 2023. https://www.quoteslyfe.com/quote/Our-Age-of-Anxiety-is-in-great-47111

16. Basso JC, Suzuki WA. The effects of acute exercise on mood, cognition, neurophysiology, and neurochemical pathways: a review. *Brain Plasticity.* 2017;2(2):127–152. doi:10.3233/BPL-160040

17. Reed K. 30 Self-care quotes so you can give the world the best of you. n.d. Accessed February 20, 2023. https://healingbrave.com/blogs/all/self-care-quotes

18. Ellis E, Reupert A, Hammer M. We're just touching the surface: Australian university lecturers' experiences of teaching theories of child development in early childhood teacher education programs. *Cambridge Journal of Education.* 2022;52(6):715–733. doi:10.1080/0305764X.2022.2047892

19. Siegel D. *The Developing Mind: Toward a Neurobiology of Interpersonal Experience.* Guilford Press; 1999.

20. Galinski E. AZ Quotes. n.d. Accessed February 12, 2023. https://www.azquotes.com/author/64289-Ellen_Galinsky

21. Perry B. The neurosequential model of therapeutics: applying principles of neuroscience to clinical work with traumatized and maltreated children. In: Webb NB, ed. *Working with Traumatized Children in Child Welfare.* Guilford Press; 2006:27–52.

22. Cozolino L. *The Social Neuroscience of Education: Optimizing Attachment and Learning in the Classroom.* W W Norton & Company; 2012.

23. Hong R, Mason CM. Becoming a neurobiologically-informed play therapist. *International Journal of Play Therapy.* 2016;25(1):35–44. doi:10.1037/pla0000020

24. Perry B, Hambrick E. The Neurosequential Model of Therapeutics. *The Journal of Strengths-Based Interventions.* 2008.

Accessed February 20, 2023. https://www.researchgate.net/publication/237346956_The_Neurosequential_Model_of_Therapeutics

25. Perry B, Winfrey O. *What Happened to You? Conversations on Trauma, Resilience, and Healing.* Pan McMillan; 2021.

26. Ray D. *A Therapist's Guide to Child Development: The Extraordinarily Normal Years.* Routledge; 2015.

27. Reynolds E, Stagnitti K, Kidd E. Play, language and social skills of children aged 4-6 years attending a play based curriculum school and a traditionally structured classroom curriculum school in low socio-economic areas. *Australasian Journal of Early Childhood.* 2011;36(4):120–130. doi:10.1177/183693911103600416

28. Dahmardeh MR, Mehdinejad V, Harfteh FSK. The effect of play education on students' emotional regulation and social relationships. *Pajouhan Scientific Journal.* 2022;20(4):277–285. doi:10.52547/psj.20.4.277

29. Petersen H, Holodynski M. Bewitched to be happy? The impact of pretend play on emotion regulation of expression in 3- to 6-Year-olds. *The Journal of Genetic Psychology.* 2020;181(2-3):11–126. doi:10.1080/00221325.2020.1734909

30. Vygotsky LS. Play and its role in the mental development of the child. *Soviet Psychology.* 1967;5(3):6–18.

31. Verma P, Yadav A, Rani S, Malik S. Biological clock vs social clock conflict in adolescents. *Journal of Applied & Natural Science.* 2021;13(1):327–342. doi:10.31018/jans.v13i1.2571

32. Shanker S. Self-regulation: the five domains. The MEHRIT Centre. n.d. Accessed April 26, 2023. https://self-reg.ca/five-domains/

33. National Center for Learning Disabilities. *The State of Learning Disabilities: Understanding the 1 in 5.* National Center for Learning Disbilities; 2017. Accessed March 2, 2023. https://www.ncld.org/research/state-of-learning-disabilities/

34. National Center for Learning Disabilities. *Forward Together: Helping Educators Unlock the Power of Students who Learn Differently.* National Center for Learning Disbilities; 2019. Accessed March 2, 2023. https://www.ncld.org/wp-content/uploads/2019/05/Forward-Together_NCLD-report.pdf

35. Anderson CJK, Klassen RM, Georgiou GK. Inclusion in Australia: what teachers say they need and what school psychologists can offer. *School Psychology International.* 2007;28(2):131–147. doi:10.1177/0143034307078086

36. Wray E, Sharma U, Subban P. Factors influencing teacher self-efficacy for inclusive education: a systematic literature review. *Teaching and Teacher Education.* 2022;117:103800. doi:10.1016/j.tate.2022.103800

37. Disability Royal Commission. *Issues Paper: Education and Learning.* Royal Commission into Violence, Abuse, Neglect and Exploitation of People with Disability; 2019. Accessed March 2, 2023. https://disability.royalcommission.gov.au/publications/education

38. Autism Spectrum Australia. Autism prevalence rate up by an estimated 40% to 1 in 70 people. 2018. Accessed March 2, 2023. https://www.autismspectrum.org.au/news/autism-prevalence-rate-up-by-an-estimated-40-to-1-in-70-people-11-07-2018

39. American Psychiatric Association. *Diagnostic and Statistical Manual of Mental Disorders (5th ed.).* American Psychiatric Association; 2013.

40. Australian Bureau of Statistics. *Disability, Ageing and Carers, Australia: Summary of Findings. 2018.* Australian Bureau of Statistics; 2019. Accessed March 3, 2023, https://www.abs.gov.au/statistics/health/disability/disability-ageing-and-carers-australia-summary-findings/2018#cite-window1

41. Raising Children Network (Australia). Thinking and learning strengths in autistic children and pre-teens. n.d. Accessed April 24 2023. https://www.altogetherautism.org.nz/strengths-and-abilities-in-autism/

43. The Royal Children's Hospital Melbourne. Attention deficit hyperactivity disorder (ADHD). n.d. Accessed February 12, 2023. https://www.rch.org.au/kidsinfo/fact_sheets/ADHD_an_overview/

44. Taylor M, O'Donoghue T, Houghton S. To medicate or not to medicate? The decision-making process of Western Australian parents following their child's diagnosis with an attention deficit hyperactivity disorder. *International Journal of Disability.* 2006;53(1):111–128. doi:10.1080/10349120500510115

45. Thapar A. ADHD: progressing from genetic discoveries to biological insights. *American Journal of Psychiatry.* 2020;177:802–804. doi:10.1176/appi.ajp.2020.20070961

46. Worsley L. *The Secret of Strong Kids: Bringing Resilience into the Common Language of Families.* 2nd Ed. The Resilience Doughnut Pty Ltd; 2006.

47. Low K. The strengths of people with ADHD. Very Well Mind. n.d. Accessed April 24, 2023, https://www.verywellmind.com/the-strengths-of-adhd-20698

48. Fitzpatrick JP, Latimer J, Olson HC, et al. Prevalence and profile of neurodevelopment and fetal alcohol spectrum disorder (FASD) amongst Australian Aboriginal children living in remote communities. *Research in Developmental Disabilities*. 2017;65:114–126. doi:10.1016/j.ridd.2017.04.001

49. Bower C, Elliott E. *Australian Guide to the Diagnosis of Fetal Alcohol Spectrum Disorder (FASD)*. Australian Government Department of Health; 2020.

50. Reed N. Advocates of FASD students in Qld schools push for more support, prevent future 'in correctional services'. 2021. Accessed April 20, 2023. https://www.abc.net.au/news/2021-03-09/fetal-alcohol-spectrum-disorder-petition-recognition-schools/13226610

51. O'Connor MJ, Portnoff LC, Lebsack-Coleman M, Dipple KM. Suicide risk in adolescents with fetal alcohol spectrum disorders. *Birth Defects Research*. 2019;11(12):822–828. doi:https://doi.org/10.1002/bdr2.1465

52. POPFASD. Deb Evenson & Jan Lutke's Eight Magic Keys. 1997. Accessed March 2, 2023. https://static.fasdoutreach.ca/resources/0-9/8-magic-keys/8-magic-keys.pdf

53. O'Hagan K. *Identifying Emotional and Psychological Abuse: A Guide for Childcare Professionals*. Open University Press; 2006.

54. Oberg GM, Bryce I. Australian teachers' perception of their preparedness to teach traumatised students: a systematic literature review. *Australian Journal of Teacher Education*. 2022;47(2):76–101. doi:10.14221/ajte.2022v47n2.6

55. Thomas L. What is trauma? 5 March 2019. Accessed February 25, 2023. https://professionals.childhood.org.au/prosody/2019/03/what-is-trauma/.

56. Center on the Developing Child at Harvard University. Applying the science of child development in child welfare systems. 2017. Accessed March 24, 2023, https://harvardcenter.wpenginepowered.com/wp-content/uploads/2016/10/HCDC_ChildWelfareSystems_rev2017.pdf

57. Centres of Disease Control and Prevention. About the CDC-Kaiser ACE Study. n.d. Accessed March 4, 2023, https://www.cdc.gov/violenceprevention/aces/about.html

58. Ayre K, Krishnamoorthy G. *Trauma-informed Behaviour Support: A Practical Guide to Developing Resilient Learners*. University of Southern Queensland; 2020. Accessed April 1, 2023. https://open.umn.edu/opentextbooks/textbooks/936

59. van der Kolk B. Developmental Trauma Disorder. *Psychiatric Annals*. 2005;35(5):401–408. Accessed April 1, 2023. https://doi.org/10.3928/00485713-20050501-06

60. NSW Government: Communities and Justice. Child at risk of harm and neglect. n.d. Accessed April 26, 2023. https://www.facs.nsw.gov.au/families/Protecting-kids/reporting-child-at-risk/harm-and-neglect/chapters/signs-of-abuse

61. Conching AKS, Thayer Z. Biological pathways for historical trauma to affect health: a conceptual model focusing on epigenetic modifications. *Social Science*. 2019;230:74–82. doi:10.1016/j.socscimed.2019.04.001

62. NSW Migration Heritage Centre. Child migration to Australia. n.d. Accessed March 4 2023. https://www.migrationheritage.nsw.gov.au/exhibition/fairbridge-farm-school/child-migration-to-australia/index.html

63. Dodson S. Intergenerational trauma: why many First Nations people in Australia can't simply 'get over it' and 'move on'. Australians

Together. 2023. Accessed March 4, 2023. https://australianstogether. org.au/discover-and-learn/the-wound/intergenerational-trauma/

64. Bottoms T. *Conspiracy of Silence: Queensland's Frontier Killing Times*. Allen & Unwin; 2013.

65. Menzies K. Understanding the Australian Aboriginal experience of collective, historical and intergenerational trauma. *International Social Work*. 2019;62(6):1522–1534. doi:10.1177/0020872819870585

66. Milroy H. A call on practitioners to play a stronger role in Intergenerational Trauma. *Intergenerational Trauma Blog*. 2018. Accessed March 3, 2023. https://croakey.org/a-call-on-practitioners-to-play-a-stronger-role-on-intergenerational-trauma/

67. Queensland Government. Aboriginal and Torres Strait Island people: Communities: Normanton. Queensland Government. n.d. Accessed March 4, 2023. https://www.qld.gov.au/ firstnations/cultural-awareness-heritage-arts/community-histories/ community-histories-n-p/community-histories-normanton

68. Queensland Government. Aboriginal and Torres Strait Island peoples: Communities: Mapoon. Queensland Government. n.d. Accessed March 4, 2023. https://www.qld.gov.au/firstnations/ cultural-awareness-heritage-arts/community-histories/ community-histories-m/community-histories-mapoon

69. Glazzard J, Rose A. The impact of teacher well-being and mental health on pupil progress in primary schools. *Journal of Public Mental Health*. 2020;19(4):349–357. doi:10.1108/ JPMH-02-2019-0023

70. White J, Gardner J. *Classroom X-Factor: The Power of Body Language and Non-verbal Communication in Teaching*. Routledge; 2011.

71. Cummin R, Ning L, Mark W, Mark S. A demonstration of set-points for subjective wellbeing. *Journal of Happiness Studies.* 2014; 15(1):183. doi:10.1007/s10902-013-9444-9

72. Le Messurier M. *Guiding Kids Through the Tough Moments: Techniques to Build a Space Where Children Can Thrive.* 1st ed. Routledge; 2023.

73. Delahooke M. *Beyond Behaviours: Using Brain Science and Compassion to Understand and Solve Behavioural Challenges.* John Murray Press; 2019.

74. Siegel DJ, Payne Bryson T. *The Whole-brain Child: 12 Revolutionary Strategies to Nurture your Child's Developing Mind.* Scribe Publications; 2012.

75. Brach T. Quotes about biochemical. Quote Master. n.d. Accessed March 11, 2023, https://www.quotemaster.org/Biochemical

76. Rogers C. The necessary and sufficient conditions of therapeutic personality change. *Journal of Consulting Psychology.* 1957;21(2):95–103. doi:10.1037/h0045357

77. Boyd S. Connection's key! 14 Quotes for raising strong kids. Youth Dynamics. n.d. Accessed March 3, 2023. https://www.youthdynamics. org/connections-key-14-quotes-for-raising-strong-kids/

78. Schmidt Hasson J. *Safe, Seen, and Stretched in the Classroom: The Remarkable Ways Teachers Shape Students' Lives.* Taylor & Francis Group; 2021.

79. Golding K, Fain J, Frost A, et al. *Observing Children with Attachment Difficulties in School: A Tool for Identifying and Supporting Emotional and Social Difficulties in Children Aged 5–11.* Jessica Kingsley Publishing; 2013.

80. Badenoch B. *The Heart of Trauma: Healing the Embodied Brain in the Context of Relationships.* W.W Norton & Company; 2017.

81. Bomber L. *Inside I am Hurting: Practical Strategies for Supporting Children with Attachment Difficulties in School.* Worth Publishing; 2007.

82. National Scientific Council on the Developing Child. Supportive relationships and active skill-building strengthen the foundations of resilience: Working Paper No. 13. n.d. Accessed March 5, 2023, www.developingchild.harvard.edu

83. Benson J. The power of unconditional positive regard. *Educational Leadership.* 2016;73(9):22–27.

84. Hughes D. An attachment-based treatment of maltreated children and young people. *Attachment and Human Development.* 2004;6(3):263 278.

85. Anglicare Victoria. A relationship-based approach to supporting students who have experienced trauma: Resource eight. n.d. Accessed March 24, 2023. https://education.vic.gov.au/documents/school/teachers/health/146_teachar_resource8_v4.pdf

86. Maté G, Neufeld G. *Hold on to Your Kids: Why Parents Need to Matter More Than Peers.* 1st ed. Random House; 2019.

87. Jackson L, Peck S. Managing the classroom by teaching emotional regulation. *ASCD.* 2018;14(1). Accessed April 7, 2023. https://www.ascd.org/el/articles/managing-the-classroom-by-teaching-emotional-regulation

88. Graziano PA, Reavis RD, Keane SP, Calkins SD. The role of emotion regulation and children's early academic success. *Journal of School Psychology.* 2007;45(1):3–19. doi:10.1016/j.jsp.2006.09.002

89. van der Kolk B. *The Body Keeps the Score: Mind, Brain and Body in the Transformation of Trauma*. Penguin; 2015.

90. Brown B. *Atlas of the Heart: Mapping Meaningful Connection and the Language of Human Experience*. Random House; 2021.

91. Lambert MT. *The Tapping Project: Introducing Emotional Freedom Techniques (EFT) to reduce anxiety and improve well-being in primary school students*. PhD thesis. Charles Darwin University; 2020. Accessed April 13, 2023. https://researchers.cdu.edu.au/en/studentTheses/the-tapping-project

92. Stapleton P, Mackay E, Chatwin H, et al. Effectiveness of a school-based Emotional Freedom Techniques intervention for promoting student well-being. *Adolescent Psychiatry*. 2017;7(2):112–126. doi:1 0.2174/2210676607666171101165425

93. Varner E. Group drumming as a conduit to enhanced self and community relationships. *Journal of General Music Education*. 2022;35(3):28–31. doi:10.1177/27527646221079642

94. Hagen I, Skjelstad S, Nayar US. 'I just find it easier to let go of anger': reflections on the ways in which yoga influences how young people manage their emotions. *Frontiers in Psychology*, 2021;12doi:10.3389/fpsyg.2021.729588

95. de Witte M, Spruit A, van Hooren S, Moonen X, Stams G-J. Effects of music interventions on stress-related outcomes: a systematic review and two meta-analyses. *Health Psychology Review*. 2020;14(2):294–324. doi:10.1080/17437199.2019.1627897

96. Panksepp J. Can play diminish ADHD and facilitate the construction of the social brain? *Journal of the Canadian Academy of Child and Adolescent Psychiatry*. 2007;16:57–66. Accessed April 20, 2023. https://pubmed.ncbi.nlm.nih.gov/18392153/

97. Goodall E, Brownlow C, Fein EC, Candeloro S. Creating inclusive classrooms for highly dysregulated students: what can we learn from existing literature? *Education Sciences*. 2022;12(8). doi:10.3390/educsci12080504

98. Abbanat J. Regulation before education. *Alliance Against Seclusion and Restraint*. 2020. Accessed March 24, 2023. https://endseclusion.org/2020/08/17/regulation-before-education/

99. Gonluacik MC, Belenkuyu C, Tas S. Examining the relationship between teachers' emotion regulation skills and classroom management competencies. *International Online Journal of Educational Sciences*. 2022;14(5):1309–1323. doi:10.15345/iojes.2022.05.012

100. Sullivan A. Schools' tough approach to bad behaviour isn't working – and may escalate problems. *The Conversation*. May 27, 2016. Accessed March 25, 2023. https://theconversation.com/schools-tough-approach-to-bad-behaviour-isnt-working-and-may-escalate-problems-56737

101. McKay M, Wood J. *Dialectical Behavior Therapy Diary: Monitoring your Emotional Regulation Day by Day*. Harbinger Publications; 2011.

102. Sperber S. fight-or-flight response: Definition, symptoms, and examples. Berkeley Well-Being Institute. n.d. Accessed March 20, 2023, https://www.berkeleywellbeing.com/fight-or-flight.html

103. Perry B. The 3 Rs: Reaching the learning brain. Beacon House Therapeutic Services and Trauma Team. 2019. Accessed April 23, 2023. https://beaconhouse.org.uk/wp-content/uploads/2019/09/The-Three-Rs.pdf

104. Coloroso B. AZ Quotes. n.d. Accessed April 23, 2023. https://www.azquotes.com/author/64787-Barbara_Coloroso

105. Payne Bryson T. How to be assertive with your toddler. n.d. Accessed April 23, 2023. https://www.tinabryson.com/news/how-to-be-assertive-with-your-toddler

106. Landy S. *Pathways to Competence: Encouraging Healthy Social and Emotional Development in Young Children.* 2nd ed. Brookes Publishing; 2009.

107. Linehan M. *DBT Skills Training Manual.* 2nd ed. Guilford Publications; 2014.

108. Ruskin J. 95 Education quotes: Inspire children, parents, and teachers. n.d. Accessed April 23, 2023. https://www.developgoodhabits.com/education-quotes/

109. Prochaska JO, DiClemente CC. Stages and processes of self-change of smoking: toward an integrative model of change. *Journal of Consulting and Clinical Psychology.* 1983;51:390–395. doi: 10.1037//0022-006x.51.3.390

ABOUT THE AUTHOR

Anne Maree is proud to be the daughter of George and Patricia Lister and is the second eldest of their six children. She spent her early life in Roma and then moved to Redcliffe in Year 9 with her family. Anne Maree was not a city kid and left school at sixteen to return to Roma as a trainee enrolled nurse. In search of adventure, she moved to Cloncurry, where she met her husband, and worked as a nurse until just before having her second child. Suffering from depression after the birth of her second child and living in a Main Roads camp with few interests outside of looking after her two young children, she decided to complete senior science and maths subjects to improve her mental health. In high school, the girls of her era were actively discouraged from undertaking a complete maths/science course, so this was some unfinished business. Anne Maree got a strong sense of satisfaction in completing these subjects with good marks as an adult – and she has not stopped studying since. A favourite saying is, 'There is so much to learn and so little time.'

Anne Maree started studying for a Certificate in Youth Work by distance education through James Cook University because, despite having significant knowledge, she found her workplace did not take her views seriously as she did not have a university degree. As she studied and had success, she transferred into higher level courses – firstly, a Bachelor of Community Welfare and then a Bachelor of Social Work, and then into the Honours program, completing a thesis on the wellbeing of young people in high school from the perspectives of teachers. Anne Maree presented this thesis to the Suicide Prevention Conference in Cairns.

While working in Cape York as a case worker for Youth Justice, she felt out of her depth with the number of young people who had either attempted suicide or had witnessed the suicide of a friend or family member – and so she undertook a Master of Suicidology to improve her competence. Later in her career, when counselling children at schools, she completed a Graduate Diploma in Therapeutic Play to meet the needs of the children she was working with. Currently, she is studying for a Diploma in Creative Arts and Health as she sees creative therapies as a gentle approach to healing and something that will gain more acceptance from the medical community in future years.

Anne Maree is particularly interested in the neurobiology of the brain and how we can use this knowledge in our everyday interactions to improve children's sense of safety, connections to others, and learning. She is fascinated by the wisdom evident in First Nations' cultural practices and traditions throughout the world, which match with what neuroscience is now discovering. Anne Maree is passionate about preventing developmental trauma and educating about the long-term implications of adverse childhood experiences with the dream that one day, we will have a much greater focus on preventing and healing trauma in our communities.

Anne Maree lives in Normanton and has four adult children and a much-loved grandchild. She provides counselling to children at schools in the surrounding area and strongly believes in the power of unconditional positive regard, which is a constant in her work. Her hope for this book is that it provides teachers with different ways to see and manage emotional storms in their classrooms, resulting in a love of learning for the most vulnerable students and a continued love of teaching for those entrusted with their education.

ADDITIONAL RESOURCES

Go to https://www.strong-kids.com.au/contact to request a free copy of the resources 'What Strategies When' or 'Calm Seas' to help you implement the strategies in this book. You will also find lots of other free resources on this page https://www.strong-kids.com.au.

Tips for Calm Seas

C
- Connection
- Curiosity
- Calm approach
- Co-Regulation
- Consistency
- Courage
- Compassion

S
- STOP Strategy
- Skill development focus
- Strengths Approach
- Storm Spotting - notice states

A
Awareness of
- Developmental stages
- Neurodiversity
- Trauma and ACEs
- The impact of dominant discourses and culture

E
- Establish regulation activities as a daily plan
- Empower students to use regulation skills
- Educate about the brain & regulation states

L
- Learn and lead whole-of-class regulation.
- Lifeboats - notice when needed and distribute as required.

A
- Acknowledge emotions 'name it to tame it'.
- Advocate for students' needs within the system
- Acceptance of things we cannot change

M
- Meet sensory needs
- Model regulation
- Mindfulness
- Movement
- Music and Rhythm

S
- Self-care
- Self-care
- Self-care!

In the Classroom

Anne Maree Taney
https://www.strong-kids.com.au

181

NOTES

NOTES

Made in the USA
Monee, IL
19 January 2025

10067204R10107